147,

D1130654

DANKMAR ADLER

HIS THEATRES AND AUDITORIUMS

DANKMAR ADLER

DANKMAR ADLER

HIS THEATRES AND AUDITORIUMS

BY CHARLES E. GREGERSEN, A.I.A.
with a biography of Dankmar Adler
prepared in collaboration with
JOAN W. SALTZSTEIN

assisted by Susan Wolfson

Swallow Press
Ohio University Press
Athens

Library of Congress Cataloging-in-Publication Data

Gregersen, Charles E.
    Dankmar Adler : his theatres and auditoriums / by
Charles E. Gregersen ; with a biography of Dankmar Adler
prepared in collaboration with Joan W. Saltzstein ; assisted
by Susan Wolfson.
      p.   cm.
    Includes bibliographical references.
    ISBN 0-8040-0928-7
    1. Adler, Dankmar, 1844–1900—Catalogs.
2. Theaters—United States—Construction—Catalogs.
3. Auditoriums—United States—Catalogs.
4. Architecture, Modern—19th century—United States—
Catalogs. I. Saltzstein, Joan W. II. Wolfson, Susan.
III. Title.
NA737.A29A4   1989
725′.83′092—dc20   89-27547
                                                      CIP

Swallow Press/Ohio University Press books are printed on
acid-free paper. ∞

To my wife, Barbara, and my aunt, Eva Lind

CONTENTS

LIST OF ILLUSTRATIONS

Frontispiece: Dankmar Adler. Memorial page by Louis H. Sullivan from *The Inland Architect and News Record*, May 1900. (Art Institute of Chicago)

PREFACE

Dankmar Adler's most important contribution to the history of architecture is the body of acoustically successful theaters and auditoriums he designed. Although he also made significant contributions to the development of the skyscraper and the architectural profession, sadly, he is most often remembered only as the mentor of his internationally renowned partner, Louis H. Sullivan.

The late Richard Nickel suggested this disservice to Dankmar Adler's memory could best be rectified with a book on Adler's acoustical theories after he read a paper I prepared on the subject in 1966, my last year at the Illinois Institute of Technology. I did not give it serious consideration until Nickel introduced me to the late Joan W. Saltzstein, Adler's granddaughter, who graciously agreed to assist on the project.

The research and editing of this book was funded by grants from the Graham Foundation for Advanced Studies in the Fine Arts. At the suggestion of the foundation's director, Carter H. Manny, Jr., I was introduced to the late Lyle F. Yerges, a noted expert in the field of acoustics. Mr. Yerges had long been an admirer of Adler's approach to acoustical design which he had come to understand through his involvement in the restoration of Adler's greatest achievement, the Auditorium Theatre. Over the years, he offered me invaluable insights into Adler's work as well as great assistance in the preparation of the book.

I am indebted to Susan Wolfson whose faith in the manuscript led to its publication, and who patiently labored to assure that the text was logical and clearly understandable. I am also indebted to Dr. Paul E. Sprague, architectural historian and scholar of the work of Adler & Sullivan, who helped me organize the manuscript.

I was assisted by my wife, Barbara, who typed my notes and the various drafts, and by Timothy J. Samuelson, architectural historian, who undertook much of the research. Throughout the preparation of this book, we were assisted by numerous other individuals. Special thanks are due to Annette Fern, Cecelia Chin, and Mary Woolever, of the Burnham Library of the Art Institute of Chicago; Julia Westerberg of the Chicago Historical Society; Alexis Praus of the Kalamazoo Public Museum; Irma Strauss, architectural historian; John Vinci of the Richard Nickel Committee; and to Charles Simmons and Paul Petraitis, who prepared many of the photographs. I would also like to thank Erik and Ingrid Gregersen and Bonnie de-Noyelles for their proofreading assistance.

Charles E. Gregersen, A.I.A.
October 12, 1988

DANKMAR ADLER

HIS THEATRES AND AUDITORIUMS

Dankmar Adler—
A Biographical Sketch

D ankmar Adler was born and spent his early childhood in Stadt Lengsfeld, a small town near Eisenach in what is now East Germany, where his family had lived for generations. Both his grandfather, Judah, and his father, Liebman, were well respected rabbis and teachers. Liebman had married Dankmar's mother Sara Eliel, the daughter of a tanner from the neighboring town of Nentershausen, in August of 1843. Sara died shortly after her son's birth on July 3, 1844. The grieving father, according to family tradition, named the baby Dankmar, a combination of the German "dank" or thanks and the Hebrew "mar" or bitter—bitterness at the loss of the mother, thanks for the birth of a son.[1]

Two years later, Liebman married Zerlina Picard, a woman fifteen years his junior. Although she bore thirteen children, she remained a devoted mother to Dankmar throughout her long life.

In 1854, restrictions and persecution drove the Adler family to join the many who sought freedom in America. Liebman, his wife and five children emigrated to Detroit, where Liebman became rabbi of Temple Beth El.

Dankmar was educated in the public schools of Detroit and Ann Arbor but failed to pass his entrance examinations to the University of Michigan. His father decided to employ architect John Schaefer to introduce Adler to the practice of architecture, because he had earlier shown some aptitude for drawing during a course of instruction under Jules Melchers, a modeler and sculptor.

In the spring of 1861, Rabbi Adler was called to serve the K.A.M. (Kehilath Anshe Mayriv) Temple in Chicago where he remained to the end of his life. In Chicago, Dankmar Adler soon entered the office of August Bauer, a prominent architect of German birth who had begun his American career working with Carstensen and Gildermeister on the New York Crystal Palace of 1853.

Adler's employment with Bauer was cut short in July of 1862 by his enlistment in the First Regiment of the Illinois Light Artillery. He saw service in Kentucky, Tennessee, and Georgia from 1862 to 1864, and participated in some of the hardest fought battles of the Civil War. Although wounded, he escaped serious injury and illness. During the last nine months of his army career, he was attached to the Topographical Engineer's Office of the Military Division of Tennessee as a draftsman where he received much of his engineering experience. He later wrote, "I made as good use of my time and was well equipped for my life's work as if my studies had been pursued at home."[2]

After his discharge from the Army, Adler returned to Bauer's office. Bauer, however, sneered at Adler's army career, which he considered a waste of time, and so offended the young apprentice that Adler left his office and joined that of Ozia S. Kinney, an architect with a sizable practice in religious and institutional work throughout the Midwest. He soon became foreman, a position he held until Kinney's death in 1869.

By May of that year he entered into partnership with Kinney's son, Ashley J., and the firm became known as Kinney & Adler. Of this firm's works, the Main Building at the College of Wooster (1867–70) at Wooster, Ohio; the First Methodist Church (1867–69) at Kalamazoo, Michigan; the Wilcoxon Opera House (1868–69) at Freeport, Illinois; and the waterworks (1870) and Second Presbyterian Church (1869–71) at La Porte, Indiana were all constructed under Adler's direction.

In January of 1871, after he severed his connection with Ashley J. Kinney, Adler entered into partnership with Edward Burling, a prominent Chicago architect a number of years his senior. The exact nature of the relationship is unclear. The two principals were listed throughout the decade in the city directories as if a partnership did not exist. Work done in their office is variously attributed to E. Burling & Co.; Burling & Adler; Burling, Adler & Co.; and to E. Burling, but as yet none has been found attributed only to Adler. For the sake of convenience, this book assumes this was a real partnership and refers to it as Burling & Adler.

In the Great Fire of October 1871, most of Chicago's central business district and North Side were destroyed, which led to a building boom that soon found the firm, "counting their work by the miles of frontage."[3] Under this heavy work load Adler appears usually to have found himself either supervising the preparation of drawings or the construction of buildings, so only a few of the firm's buildings were actually designed by him. Among the more prominent of these were: the Methodist Church Block (1871-73), the First National Bank (1871), the Kingsbury Music Hall (1872-73), all in Chicago; the First Congregational Church (1873-74) in Oak Park, Illinois; and the Sinai Temple (1875-76) in Chicago. In the latter two, where the architectural embellishments appear to have been designed by John H. Edelmann,[4] Adler established the practice characteristic of most of his later works—he defined the program, developed the general concept of the building and then left this naked form, as it were, in the hands of another to clothe.

Adler married Dila Kohn, the daughter of a Chicago pioneer, Abraham Kohn, in 1872. Kohn had arrived in America from Germany in 1844. He came to Chicago in 1846 and opened a small clothing store. He became a prominent Republican and was City Clerk under the colorful Chicago mayor "Long John" Wentworth. He was one of the founders of the K.A.M. Temple. The Adlers had three children: Abraham, born in 1872; Sidney, in 1876; and Sara,[5] in 1877.

Burling and Adler terminated their partnership very early in 1879, probably because of the extremely bad publicity Burling was receiving at the time. He had been accused of incompetence in administration of his duties as superintendent of construction of the Customs House in Chicago, for which he was brought to trial and eventually acquitted.[6]

At the time of its dissolution, the firm was about to undertake the construction of a fairly substantial concert hall to be known as the Central Music Hall in honor of its principal tenant, The Rev. David Swing's Central Church. This project was the brainchild of George B. Carpenter, a local promoter of concerts and lectures and a member of the church. Carpenter first contacted Burling & Adler about his proposed building in 1876. Later Carpenter would recount that he had personally undertaken extensive research into the problem, which involved visits to all of the major halls in America and a study of the plans of all the major European houses, and, on the basis of this research, Adler had prepared six different schemes for the project.[7] The Central Music Hall was the first of Adler's auditoriums in which it was apparent the design was based primarily on acoustical principles. It would seem likely, therefore, that it was Carpenter's research which provided much of the information on acoustics that would later make Adler famous. In summing up his life's work, Adler referred to the Central Music Hall as, "the foundation of whatever professional standing I may have acquired."[8] The hall's superb acoustical qualities were immediately recognized, and Adler established a warm friendship with several of its influential backers. These contacts eventually led to a number of his most important commissions.

Adler hired Louis H. Sullivan as his foreman and chief designer, apparently on May 1, 1880. On May 1, 1882, Sullivan became Adler's junior partner in the firm of D. Adler & Co. Exactly one year later Adler promoted Sullivan to a full partner, and the famous firm of Adler & Sullivan was born. From the beginning of their association in 1880 until the dissolution of the partnership in 1895, Sullivan assumed primary responsibility for the aesthetic aspects of most of Adler's buildings.

Most of the firm's work in the years after the completion of the Central Music Hall was relatively modest. Although Sullivan's hand is usually evident, none is architecturally noteworthy. The Borden Residence (1881–82), the Hammond Library (1882–83), the Troescher Building (1884), all in Chicago; the Academy of Music (1881–82) at Kalamazoo, Michigan; and the Aurora Watch Company (1883–84) at Aurora, Illinois are typical examples. Also among the works of this period was the residence at 3543 S. Ellis Avenue in Chicago (the center of three adjoining row houses), erected in 1885, where Adler lived the rest of his life.

In 1885, the firm of Adler & Sullivan was retained by the Chicago Opera Festival Association (a number of the directors, including its president, Ferdinand W. Peck, were members of Rev. Swing's Central Church) to remodel the interior of the Interstate Industrial Exposition Building on the lakefront into an opera house which seated over 6,000 people for a two-week festival of grand opera. The success of this festival convinced the members of the Opera Festival Association that Chicago could support a large permanent hall suitable not only for operatic but also for choral and orchestral performances, and the way in which Adler had so skillfully overcome all the difficulties of remodeling the Exposition Building convinced Peck in particular that Adler should be its architect.

Adler and Sullivan began work on preliminary designs for the building, which was to be called the Chicago Auditorium, in the summer of 1886. Their appointment as architects was not actually confirmed until Peck and his associates held their first meetings as directors of the Chicago Auditorium Association in December of that year. From then until completion of the Auditorium over three years later, the relatively obscure firm was faced with the unprecedented task of designing the largest public building in America and the particularly vexing problems of unifying three totally unrelated functions: theatre, hotel, and office building.

The Auditorium Association sent Adler to Europe, in the summer of 1888, to procure the best available equipment for the stage of the Auditorium. This gave him the opportunity to improve greatly his knowledge of contemporary developments in theatre design. The journey led him through England, France, Germany, and Austria-Hungary, where he was able to examine a number of the best known theatres of the day,[9] and ended in Vienna, where he ordered equipment and designs for an elaborate hydraulically operated stage.

The opening of the Auditorium Theatre on December 9, 1889, was the social event of the year. President Benjamin Harrison and Vice President Levi Morton were among the many distinguished guests present, but the high point of the evening was Adelina Patti's rendition of *Home Sweet Home*. The next evening the Auditorium began its illustrious forty-year history as the home of grand opera in Chicago when Patti appeared in Gounod's *Romeo and Juliet*. Adler's brilliant solution to the functional and mechanical problems and his partner's beautiful decorative scheme brought the firm instant fame.

Adler's greatest achievements in the years after the completion of the Chicago Auditorium were the first use of setbacks in the design of the Schiller (later Garrick) Theater Building (1891–92) in Chicago, and the first use of caisson foundations in office building construction under the Chicago Stock Exchange (1893–94). Among other important buildings executed by the firm during this period were the Wainwright Building (1890–91) in St. Louis, the Transportation Building at the World's Columbian Exposition (1891–93) in Chicago, and the Guaranty (1894–96) (later Prudential) Building in Buffalo, New York.

The relationship between Adler and Sullivan was cordial and warm throughout the years of their partnership. Sullivan was frequently a guest in the Adler home and had great rapport with the children. Although most of the firm's clients were Adler's, he went out of his way to promote and praise his partner. Whatever their differences in personality, there was no hint of a rift between the two men.

It came as a great surprise to the architectural profession when on July 16, 1895, Adler left the firm to join the Crane Elevator Company as consulting architect and general manager. Adler could not resist the opportunity, as Adler & Sullivan's business had been declining. His association with the Crane Company, however, lasted only a short time. By January of the next year he had returned to the architectural profession as Dankmar Adler, Architect.

Why Adler did not try to reestablish his partnership with Sullivan is not clear, but it seems likely that it was a mutually agreed upon decision. Sullivan apparently felt Adler had deserted him, and Adler, a practical man, concluded that (at least in the short term) a revived partnership was still unlikely to succeed. By the late 1890s, the fame which both Adler and Sullivan had enjoyed barely a decade before had vanished, the victim of the triumph of neoclassicism at the Columbian Exposition in 1893. Of the few commissions Adler still received, the Isaiah Temple (1898-99) in Chicago is the best example.

Adler wrote for various architectural publications. His most noteworthy papers are: "The Paramount Requirements of a Large Opera House," 1887; "The Chicago Auditorium," 1892; "Some Notes on Earlier Chicago Architects," 1892; "Tall Office Buildings—Past and Future," 1892; "Light in Tall Office Buildings," 1892; "Theater [*sic*] Building for American Cities," 1894; "Convention Halls," 1895; and "Influence of Steel Construction and of Plate Glass upon the Development of Modern Style," 1896. One of his most important papers, "The Theatre," was still in a working draft and unfortunately not published due to his untimely death. It appears in its entirety in the appendix of this book.

Throughout his career, Adler devoted much time to the affairs of the architectural profession. He became first treasurer of the Western Association of Architects when it was founded in 1884 and a year later was elected its second president. He was a member of the Chicago Chapter of the American Institute of Architects and of the Illinois State Association of Architects. He served as president of the latter in 1886-87. When these two organizations merged in 1890 to form the Illinois Chapter of the A.I.A., he was elected treasurer of the new organization. His most lasting legacy to the profession was the legislation he drafted that resulted in the formation of the Illinois State Board of Examiners of Architects in 1898 (the first of its kind in the nation) and to which the governor appointed him as its first chairman.

Adler's home life continued to delight him, especially the marriage of his daughter Sara to Julius E. Weil in 1897 and the birth of his first grandson Edward Weil in 1899. Although he had always been quite healthy, Dankmar Adler suffered a stroke on April 6, 1900 from which he died ten days later at the age of fifty-six. He was buried in Mount Mayriv Cemetery, Chicago, where his grave is appropriately marked by one of the polished granite columns from the entrance to the Central Music Hall which was demolished in that year.

Joan W. Saltzstein
Charles E. Gregersen

1. The name was not unknown in the region, and in fact, a town named Dankmarsheim is not far from Stadt Lengsfeld.
2. Autobiography of Dankmar Adler, unpublished manuscript in Newberry Library.
3. Ibid.
4. In 1873, Edelmann, who later introduced Louis Sullivan to Adler, was employed as chief draftsman by Burling & Adler, for whom he is known to have designed the Eli Bates residence in Chicago. The similarity of the details of this building as well as those of a competition design by Edelmann of 1874 for the Plymouth Congregational Church in Chicago to the details of the First Congregational Church and Sinai Temple is evidence that Edelmann was responsible for the latter two. Although Edelmann was not employed by Burling & Adler at the time the Sinai Temple was designed, it is known that Edelmann drew a detail of its ornament in Sullivan's *Lotos Club Notebook* and that Sullivan (who worked for Edelmann at that time) designed the painted ornamentation of the synagogue's interior.
5. The mother of Joan W. Saltzstein, coauthor of this biography.
6. Details of this trial were published at length in the Chicago newspapers for the first half of 1879.
7. *The Chicago Times*, March 2, 1879.
8. Autobiography of Dankmar Adler (see 2. above).
9. His observations on these theatres may be found in "Stage Mechanisms," *The Building Budget*, February, 1889, Pp. 21–22 and in the letters that he wrote to his wife, which are now in the Newberry Library, Chicago.

ADLER'S THEATRES
AND AUDITORIUMS

Although Adler is credited with other noteworthy accomplishments, it was primarily his unique and eminently successful approach to the problems of auditorium design that established his reputation and determined the course and success of his architectural practice. His writings on the subject and the auditoriums demonstrate, contrary to what one might expect after examination of the dismal record of others in the field, that his approach was not esoteric but direct, based upon keen observation and logic. Adler was not, as often implied, only a competent engineer, he was also an architect. Adler's theatres and auditoriums are not simply monuments to his approach and its evolution, but many are important architectural monuments as well.

The first auditoriums with whose design or construction Adler was associated were the First Methodist Church (1867–69) at Kalamazoo, Michigan; the Main Building at the College of Wooster (1867–70) at Wooster, Ohio; the Wilcoxon Opera House (1868–69) at Freeport, Illinois; and the Second Presbyterian Church (1869–71) at La Porte, Indiana, all completed during his partnership with Ashley J. Kinney. The first two were completed in accordance with designs prepared before the death of Kinney's father, Ozia S. Kinney. It is still open to debate who was responsible for the design of the Wilcoxon Opera House, but the church at La Porte appears to have been entirely designed by Adler. These auditoriums were much alike, following prototypes established by the elder Kinney. Each was a rather plain rectangular, almost box-like room, which revealed no particular knowledge of acoustics on the part of their designers except for a rather correct comprehension of the problem of arranging seating.

Ideally, all seating should be centered on the source of sound, but the elder Kinney apparently recognized that such an arrangement could easily result in the focusing of sound waves back upon their source, which would produce distinct echoes. In most of these auditoriums the main floor seating was therefore centered around a point on or behind the rear wall of the stage or speaker's platform. Although there is not sufficient evidence to confirm it, it seems likely that Kinney would have centered the balcony seating of a theatre like the Wilcoxon Opera House at a point well in front of the stage apron in deference to tradition. Be that as it may, Adler followed both practices, without exception, to the end of his career.

Of all the public halls and religious buildings erected by the partnership of Burling & Adler, Adler claimed to have designed only the Methodist Church Block (1871-73) and the Sinai Temple (1875-76), both in Chicago. A contemporary source[1] also credits him with the design of the Kingsbury Music Hall (1872-73) in Chicago and its subsequent remodeling into the New Chicago Theatre (1875). On the basis of their similarity in both external and internal arrangement to the work of Kinney & Adler, one can also assign to Adler the responsibility for much of the design of the Unity Church (1872-73) in Chicago and the First Congregational Church (1873-74) in Oak Park, Illinois.

In general these auditoriums looked much like those which Adler had either designed or completed during his association with the Kinneys. Unlike them, however, the plan of the Unity Church is not rectangular. At the east end, where the pulpit was originally located, it terminates in a half octagon. Whether this feature is a leftover from the previous building (portions of which had survived the Chicago Fire and were incorporated in the new structure) is not known, but it is characteristic of all of Adler's later synagogues and concert halls including the Kingsbury Music Hall. Acoustically this arrangement was certainly more desirable than that which Adler had previously used, where anyone seated in the far corners to either side of a speaker would have been well out of sight of his face and, therefore, somewhat out of range of his voice.

As mentioned in the previous chapter, the Central Music Hall (designed by Adler while he was still Burling's partner but erected after the dissolution of their partnership and completed in 1880) was the first of his auditoriums to be designed purely on the basis of acoustical principles, most of which he seems to have culled from the research of George B. Carpenter, its chief promoter. The most important of these principles, and that which would form the basis of all of Adler's later work in the field of acoustical design, was the then rather well-known principle of the *isacoustic curve* promulgated by the noted engineer John Scott Russell (1808–82) in 1838.[2] Russell had concluded that, because sound, like light, travels in straight lines, it is necessary for all members of an audience to have an equally clear view of the source of sound in an auditorium if they are to hear it easily. Therefore, the location within an auditorium from which each member of the audience receives direct sound (as opposed to reflected sound which is usually weaker) becomes of primary importance in auditorium design. Russell realized the chief obstruction to the transmission of direct sound to any member of an audience was the head of the person seated in front of him. To overcome this defect he proposed that the floors of auditoriums be given a rise sufficiently high for every member of the audience to have an equally clear view of the source of sound. This rise would of its nature always form a curve, hence the term *isacoustic curve*.

Russell's recommendations on how to apply this principle were, however, of little use to Adler, because they were applicable only to an academic lecture hall of his day in which the lecturer stood at a fixed point. For the Central Music Hall and the other theatres and auditoriums that followed it, where the source of sound was generally spread over a large area and the audience had to be seated comfortably, Adler had to develop his own method of applying this principle, which in later years he commented on as follows:

. . . a modification of Scott Russell's isacoustic curve should be used in laying out the banking of the seats. This modification is for the purpose of obtaining an isoptic line, and consists in lowering the level of the focus to which the curves are drawn from the level of a speaker's mouth to the floor line at the front of the stage and in substituting for a single focus at the middle of the stage, foci tending toward the side of the curtain opening for the respective sides of the house so that the focus of the curve for the seats nearest any one side is at the corresponding jamb of the curtain opening.[3]

In working out this curve, the rise of the seats may become steeper than is compatible with fixed conditions as found in some houses. In such cases it becomes necessary to make adaptations which bring the total rise within the available limits of space. Drawing the sight lines over every second head instead of over every head, is one of the possible modifications and as an auxiliary to this expedient for reducing the rise of the banks, as also setting the seats alternately behind each other, so that each spectator sees between and not over the heads of those immediately before him.[4]

Observation of existing conditions teaches that if the audience is to be comfortable, the width of the seats should be from twenty inches upward and their distance from back to back from thirty-two or thirty-three inches upward, and that upon floors which have high steppings the distance from back to back should be greater than where the floor is more nearly level.[5]

When this modified *isacoustic curve* is used, in order to avoid too steep and unclimbable a rise in the balconies and galleries of an auditorium, it is necessary to start them much further back from the stage apron than is required when the more common (but less desirable) practice of staggering seating is used to plot the rise. This factor, combined with Adler's desire to bring balcony and gallery seating as close to the stage as possible and still give a full view of the proscenium from the farthest seats beneath them, resulted in the very desirable situation (seldom found in modern theatres) where the lap of one level of seating over that below is relatively slight.

The relatively low ceiling of the Central Music Hall and its division into panels by heavy beams, as well as the presence of heavy pilasters along its walls, indicate Adler had become aware of the paramount importance of controlling the volume of an auditorium to obtain proper but not excessive reverberation and of breaking up the wall and ceiling surfaces in order to diffuse the reflection of sound off these surfaces. This prevented the formation of echoes and excessive reverberation.[6]

Aside from the application of these important principles to its design, the Central Music Hall auditorium did not differ significantly in appearance from its more conventional predecessor, the Kingsbury Music Hall. Both were rather long and narrow with prominent "horseshoe" balconies (one in the Kingsbury and two in the Central Music Hall) along the side and rear walls, and each had the three-sided stage end first used by Adler in the Unity Church. They were also both illuminated during the day by a stained glass skylight which ran the length of the hall, a feature that Adler used only once again (in a modified form) in his greatest work, the Chicago Auditorium.

The success of the Central Music Hall immediately led to the commission to design the Grand Opera House in Chicago. Despite its pretentious name, this theatre, which opened in September of 1880, was only of average size. It was not an entirely new building but rather a rear addition (which housed the auditorium and stage) and interior remodeling of an existing structure that dated back to 1872. The work done by Adler and his newly employed foreman, Louis H. Sullivan, was therefore limited to the construction of the auditorium and its entrances and exits.

The seating was arranged by Adler in accordance with the modified *isacoustic curve* principle and Kinney's system of centering. Like the Central Music Hall, it had two "horseshoe" balconies carried near their fronts on cast iron columns, but the house was much shallower. The greater depth of the Central Music Hall, which provided sufficient volume and (therefore) reverberation for orchestral and choral performances, would not have been appropriate for dramatic performances in the Grand Opera House. There, intimacy with the stage and distinct audibility were essential. At either side of the stage, as was typical in most theatres of the day, were two levels of proscenium boxes. The ceiling was divided by projecting beams, as it was in the Central Music Hall, but in the latter the ceiling remained relatively level, and here it became progressively lower as it approached the stage until it coincided with the top of the proscenium.

The result of this rather modest break with tradition (which up to that time had generally resulted in the use of a domed ceiling) was an auditorium that expanded both horizontally and vertically (even though somewhat tentatively) outward from the proscenium. In later years, after refinements to this innovation led him to develop a totally new prototype for theatre design, Adler gave this rationale for using it:

> The breath, which blown directly into the air through the puckered lips will produce but a very faint sound, audible only to a distance of but a few feet, will carry thousands of feet when projected through the trumpet. So also if the sounds produced upon the stage are, as in the trumpet or as in the speaking tube, held together at the proscenium opening, and are not permitted to diffuse themselves in any direction excepting that of the audience, —if the wall surface and the ceiling are so formed as to hold in the sounds, and to carry and deflect them to the ears of the audience,— then a greater number of people can hear distinctly in the same room than under any other conditions.
>
> The practical applications of this principle gives an auditorium approximately fan shaped in plan and cuts off a number of front side seats from which but an unsatisfactory view of the stage can be obtained. But the effort to conserve the sound waves influences to a still greater extent the vertical dimensions of the auditorium. The proscenium must be low, not a foot higher than is necessary to permit full view of any possible grouping at the back of the stage from the last and highest seat in the house. If the proscenium is made higher, so much more air will have to be unnecessarily set in motion, that needlessly great efforts of speakers and singers are required if their voices are to fill the house and to reach every member of the audience. The necessity for giving reasonable head-room over balconies and galleries brings with it a gradual increase in height of ceiling from the proscenium outward. This upward tendency of the ceiling lines should be modulated into a profile which deflects the sound waves downward toward the rear of the lower portion of the house.[7]

The public's reaction to the Grand Opera House was so favorable that Adler used the design as the prototype in the next two theatre projects that followed: the Academy of Music at

Kalamazoo, Michigan, begun in 1881 and completed the next year and the remodeling of the McVicker's Theatre in Chicago, which was developed in 1883 but not executed until two years later.

Of the two, the McVicker's remodeling is the more important, because it was in this project that Adler and Sullivan (then in full partnership) became the first architects to use the electric light bulb decoratively. Rather than set the bulbs in chandeliers or brackets in the manner traditionally used for gas jets (as had been common practice since their invention in 1879), they were set directly onto the walls and ceilings against a background of ornament and became decorative features in their own right. The most elaborate application of this method of decorative lighting was to be carried out by Adler in the Chicago Auditorium several years later but was eventually rejected by him as a total means of illumination because of the objectionable glare of the bulbs.[8] The heating and ventilating system of the McVicker's was the first in any of Adler's theatres to be entirely mechanically operated.

The selection of Adler & Sullivan as architects for the temporary remodeling of the interior of the Interstate Industrial Exposition Building in Chicago into an auditorium, which was to seat over 6,000 people for the Opera Festival of 1885, was prompted not only by Adler's friendship with several of its promoters but also by the fact that he had already successfully remodeled the building for the May Festivals of 1882 and 1884 (the latter remodeling was also used for the national conventions of both the Republican and Democratic parties of that year). In these earlier remodelings of the Exposition Building, the relatively low ceiling had made it impossible to bring the entire audience close to the stage through the use of several balconies as Adler had done in his theatres. At the most, there was room for only one balcony. The excessive depth that was the inevitable result of such an arrangement forced Adler to find a new approach. In his earlier theatres he had diffused reflected sound. To allow the most remote members of the audience to hear in this deeper hall, he needed to intensify the effect of sound coming from the stage. To accomplish this, he reinforced it with sound reflected off a huge sounding board above the stage platform. In the design of the

Opera Festival Hall, Adler was again forced to adopt the same approach, but instead of the stage platform used in the earlier halls, the requirements of grand opera demanded the construction of a full stage with rigging loft and proscenium. The result was a deep, almost fan-shaped, auditorium with a huge trumpet-like proscenium that served as the sounding board.

The importance of this hall cannot be overestimated. Never before in the history of theatre design had such a large audience been comfortably seated directly in front of a proscenium. The significance of this achievement was not lost on Adler. He immediately recognized that the fan-shaped plan and trumpet-like proscenium was acoustically and aesthetically superior to the more traditional patterns he and his contemporaries had used.

It was in designing the Auditorium Theatre, the permanent successor of the Opera Festival Hall, which Adler & Sullivan began in the early summer of 1886 and continued to refine until its completion in 1889, that Adler had his first opportunity to adapt the unique features of the Opera Festival Hall to a permanent theatre. In adopting the latter's fan-shaped plan, he created the first permanent theatre in which most of the seating faced the stage directly; this departed entirely from the horseshoe or Italian opera house prototype that had dominated theatre design for over two hundred years. The Auditorium was the first major theatre where this was accomplished with more than one level of seating.[9] It is the predecessor of all modern proscenium theatres.

Adler had apparently known since his work on the Central Music Hall that with every increase in the volume of an auditorium, the likelihood of distinct echoes and other acoustical problems would increase at a disproportionate rate. As subsequent years have proven, he wisely never allowed the capacity of a theatre designed primarily for dramatic presentations to exceed 2,500, and in halls where the audibility of an individual voice was essential (such as a church, synagogue, or lecture hall), he did not permit the capacity to go much beyond 1,000. The mammoth operatic, choral, and orchestral performances planned for the Auditorium could, however, only be economically successful when presented before significantly larger audiences. He established the Auditorium's permanent capacity at 4,237 (slightly more than two-thirds that of the Opera Festival Hall). This pushed the capacity to the absolute safe limit of good acoustical design. He arranged these seats according to the prevailing classifications of the day: parquet, dress circle, boxes, main balcony, and upper and lower galleries. The capacity could originally be decreased to approximately 2,500 for dramatic presentations by lowering hinged sections of the ceiling to close off the galleries and curtaining off the rear of the balcony; or it could be increased to approximately 7,000 for conventions by extending the seating of the main floor into the foyer, reseating the boxes, and placing additional seating on the stage. This flexibility is no longer possible. The mechanical devices are now inactive due to excessive settlement of the structure (and further additions to the fixed seating would now be illegal).

The seating of the main floor and balcony is arranged according to Kinney's system of centering. In the galleries the seats are set in straight lines. Because they are so far from the stage, the angle of vision from seats at the outer walls remains fairly close to that at the center. This greatly simplified the structural system which supported the galleries and was used by Adler in all subsequent theatres.

Adler's previously cited remarks about the *isacoustic curve* imply that he applied the principle graphically. An investigation of the seating of the Auditorium Theatre (with the late Lyle Yerges) revealed that the basic isacoustic rise of its seating can be precisely calculated row by row using the following formula:

$$R = \frac{r}{d} \ D + 4''$$

Where:

> R = The total rise above the first row of seating of the front edge of a subsequent row.
>
> r = The total rise above the first row of seating at the front edge of the row immediately below that of the row being calculated.

D = The distance from the stage apron to the front edge of the row being calculated.

d = The distance from the stage apron to the front edge of the row immediately below the row being calculated.

This formula was applied to every row of seating in the Auditorium with the exception of the first 27 rows of the main floor (the entire parquet and the forward half of the dress circle) where the rise was calculated for only every other row. This compromise prevented the rise of the remaining seats from becoming excessive, and was acceptable because of the immediate proximity of these seats to the stage. To simplify construction, the *isacoustic curve* was modified into a series of straight lines. Each of the first seven rows of the main floor, for example, has a rise of 2½″ followed by six rows which each have a 3″ rise. This would have adversely affected the sight lines at the rear of each straight run if the overall curve had been followed precisely. This defect was avoided by exaggerating the curve slightly upward.

Adler had to make the Auditorium Theatre deeper because he used the *isacoustic curve* to lay out the seating. This would have been disastrous had he used a more traditional ceiling. It was imperative that the volume of the house be reduced to a minimum by lowering the ceiling as much as possible. To avoid excessive reverberation, he broke up the wall and ceiling surfaces of the forward part of the hall so reflected sound would be diffused in that area. The series of staggered elliptical vaults, which extend outward from the proscenium, is the theatre's most striking feature. Adler derived its design from the trumpet-like ceiling of the Opera Festival Hall. There were originally to have been five such vaults of equal depth. The Auditorium Association's decision, after construction began, to add a large concert organ necessitated the removal of the first of these in order to accommodate a chamber for the pipes. When the first vault (whose surface was well broken up with receding arches and engaged colonettes) was eliminated, the second vault was extended toward the proscenium to fill the void. This modification resulted in an increase of flat ceiling surface which adversely affects the acoustics of the hall and still causes annoying echoes to be heard occasionally in the front part of the parquet. By plotting the passage of sound on a schematic longitudinal section of the Auditorium as originally designed (fig. 1) as a series of straight lines from their average point of origin (a point five feet above the floor at the center of the stage), one can see that only a very small area of these staggered vaults could actually cause any sound to be reflected back into the forward part of the house.

The Auditorium was the first of Adler's theatres to be built primarily of fire resistant materials. All of the wall and ceiling surfaces are constructed of thick plaster on metal lath. The major advantage of such dense and heavy surfaces when used for acoustical value is they are non-absorptive and, therefore, do not distort or modify the sound they reflect. Because Adler preferred they not be too rigid,[10] none are apparently anchored directly to the masonry bearing walls but are attached to intermediate furring. He apparently had the walls and ceilings of all his later theatres constructed in this way.

The theatre has a large stained glass skylight similar to those used in the Kingsbury and Central Music halls. This allowed the theatre to be cleaned or used for small performances without the expense of turning on the house lights.[11] A system of winch-operated shutters in the attic above the theatre originally controlled the light during the day, and in the evening the skylight was artificially lit by electricity.

The theatre's depth and limited site (the theatre, excluding the stage, occupies a space 118'-0" wide by 178'-4" deep)

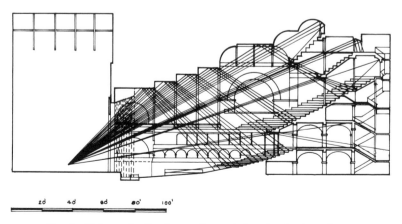

Fig. 1. Chicago Auditorium, schematic longitudinal section.

19

precluded the construction of the kind of purely monumental foyers, salons, and staircases usually associated with European opera houses of comparable size and quality. Rather than create one large foyer connected to the theatre by corridors as was common in many of these theatres, Adler butted a number of small foyers directly to the appropriate sections of seating (as always done in his small theatres). This saved space and was more convenient for the audience.

Adler believed at the time that for proper acoustics it was necessary to provide for the free flow of air at the rear of a theatre,[12] although his later theatres indicate that he eventually rejected this idea. The arrangement of foyers, the use of open stairwells in the theatre, and the complete absence of a separation between the rear of the main floor and its foyer were all used to accomplish this end.

In the design of the proscenium, Adler was faced with the difficult problem of accommodating two different proscenium widths, the larger for choral and orchestral performances and the smaller for operatic and dramatic presentations. His solution was the great hydraulically operated reducing curtain that, when lowered, cuts the width of the proscenium from 75′ to 47′.

Until the construction of the Auditorium, theatres were generally closed during July and August because no practical system existed to keep them from becoming unbearably hot. The Auditorium Association, however, wanted to be able to use the theatre during these months in order to minimize the debt. Adler and his heating consultants were forced to reexamine the problem of how to ventilate a theatre. They concluded that proper acoustics, particularly in an immense hall like the Auditorium, required the flow of air to move in the same general direction as the sound, with the size of the exhaust ducts increasing with their distance from the stage.[13] Further refinements to the kind of mechanically operated heating and ventilating system Adler first used in the McVicker's Theatre accomplished this. Fresh air is brought into the basement of the theatre through a square brick induction shaft that extends above the roof. Originally the air was washed by a shower of brine (salt water) in this shaft. In summer a great quantity of ice was used to cool the shower; in winter the salt prevented the shower from freezing. From the base of the shaft, air is forced into a system of corridor plenums under the main floor of the theatre. By manipulation of doors in these corridors, cooled air could be sent directly up the supply shafts at either side of the proscenium in summer, or in winter the air could be diverted through banks of radiators to be warmed before it entered the shafts. Above the ceiling of the theatre, the supply shafts branch into individual hemispherical plaster supply vents in the spandrel arches of the vaults and the ceiling of the upper gallery. Once inside the theatre, supply air is generally drawn down from the ceiling toward the rear of the house by exhaust fans connected by ductwork to vents in the foyers and the plenums formed by the substructure of the seating. Most of the air is exhausted under the seating at the rear of each row. Some of it is expelled through shafts that lead to the roof, while the remainder is led back into the basement plenum to be recirculated. This basic system was employed by Adler in all his later theatres.

Adler's earliest efforts at stage design had all been rather elementary because they were intended to serve the needs of the generally small and sparsely equipped traveling companies of the day. Even the huge stage of the Opera Festival Hall (126' wide by 80' deep) was of this type. For most architects, including Adler, the design of such a stage was relatively simple, because most of the equipment was actually designed and installed by experienced stage carpenters.

The problems of a stage suitable for the most elaborate productions of grand opera were totally new to Adler; little in his previous experience could have prepared him to solve them. The demands of the Auditorium Association for a mammoth theatre, hotel, and office building upon a relatively small site left a space only 62' deep by 97' wide for the stage with only a small area for scene storage and dressing rooms. The latter originally took up four floors on the north side of the stage and five floors on the south. While this was adequate for traveling companies, in later years resident companies found it cramped. Additional dressing rooms were later constructed over the adjoining alley.

The decision of the Auditorium Association to send Adler and their newly appointed stage carpenter, John Bairstow, to

Europe in the summer of 1888 to acquire suitable stage equipment seems to have been prompted by an awareness that the stage, as then projected, might not be all they desired.[14] At the conclusion of their tour, Adler and Bairstow made arrangements with the Asphalia Association in Vienna to design a completely equipped stage for the Auditorium that would follow (as a model) the system which this firm had installed several years earlier in the opera house at Budapest. Although its chief advantage was supposed to be its almost entirely incombustible iron construction, the elaborate hydraulically operated system was noted for its great flexibility and efficiency. Most of the equipment in the Auditorium was constructed in accordance with these designs by the Crane Elevator Company of Chicago, and a substantial amount (including sets) was brought directly from Vienna. The most noticeable features of the system were the cyclorama (a huge backdrop which depicted the sky under all possible weather conditions) and the flexible stage floor, operated by hydraulic rams in the two-tiered basement below. When the Auditorium Theatre opened in December of 1889, this equipment made its stage the most well-equipped in the country. Even forty years later, when the architects of the Chicago Civic Opera House returned from another European tour, they realized it remained unsurpassed.[15]

The experience gained through his work with the Asphalia Association made Adler one of the most knowledgeable men in America on the subject of stage design. His remarks, made several years after the Auditorium's completion, should be noted:

> The proscenium opening of theatres is often made so large that it must be artificially diminished in width by the insertion of imitation draperies or of bits of set scenery, for if the stage setting were made for the full width of these excessive openings, the number of people and properties and the volume of light required would exceed the means of most companies. Probably 30 feet of proscenium opening will be found ample for all theatres less than 70 feet in width between walls, and a proscenium opening from 45 to 50 feet in width will accommodate the most elaborate spectacles ever presented in this country. The proscenium opening of the Auditorium, of the Metropolitan, of the Acade-

mies in New York and Philadelphia, and that of Boston are near these figures. It is therefore not at all likely, that a proscenium opening of more than 40 feet will be required for any theatre other than the preeminently large ones before enumerated.

In the matter of the depth of stage, it would seem that it is almost impossible to give effective rendering even to parlor comedy on a stage of less depth than 25 feet, and that 40 or even 50 feet would not be an excessive depth, or one involving uneconomic results for a theatre devoted to miscellaneous performances. With reference to this matter it must be borne in mind that, for the purposes of any performance, it is much easier to cut off part of the depth of the stage by means of suitable drops than it is to add to its depth if the stage is built too shallow in the first place, and it will always be safe, in designing a theatre, to take for increase of depth of stage all the space not absolutely necessary for other purposes.

In the same way it is desirable to have as much space as possible on each side of the proscenium opening. In the absence of the large assembly rooms for actors, for chorus, ballet supers, etc. and for assembling the various people engaged in a performance as to enable them to appear promptly upon the scene. Part of this space may also be utilized for the storage of scenery, of properties, and of the baggage of traveling companies.

The height of the stage is another dimension which can hardly be made too great. Sixty or 70 feet from the stage floor to the rigging loft is not at all excessive, and 80 to 90 feet or more has been used to very good advantage. It is very desirable that it should be possible to lift the largest drops bodily without rolling, and this can only be accomplished when there is abundant height.[16]

The Chicago Auditorium, Adler's only extant theatre, represents the final step in the development of his approach to theatre design. He continued to make further refinements, but the Auditorium remained the prototype for all his later theatres. Unfortunately, he would never again have an opportunity to use his knowledge on such a grand scale.

In the spring of 1888 with the Auditorium well under way, Adler & Sullivan received the commission to design a new theatre building for Pueblo, Colorado. Known as the Grand Opera House, it was completed in the fall of 1890. Despite this theatre's relatively small size (a capacity of slightly over nine hundred), it was not designed simply as a small imitation of its predecessor, but rather it incorporated several important innovations. While the shape of the Auditorium Theatre had been determined almost exclusively by sight lines and the grid of its structural framing, in this theatre Adler defined the space through the use of purely geometric architectonic devices. The main floor was surrounded by an octagonal arcade, the dimensions of which determined the shape and size of much of the rest of the house. The numerous columns in the theatre, both structural and ornamental, unlike those in the Auditorium, never fell within areas of seating. It was the first of Adler's theatres in which all possible obstructions to vision had been eliminated. Adler devised a coffered ceiling, shaped like a half-groined vault, to achieve diffused reflections of sound in the forward part of the rather small and shallow house.

In the next few years before the dissolution of their partnership, Adler & Sullivan undertook four theatre projects: the rebuilding of the Nunnemacher Opera House in Milwaukee as the *Deutsches Stadt Theater* (a design produced early in 1890 and later turned over to another architect to execute); the remodeling of the McVicker's Theatre in Chicago after a fire in August of 1890 (primarily executed according to the lines of their previous remodeling in 1885); an unexecuted design produced in the last months of 1890 for a theatre, store, and apartment building for Seattle, Washington; and the *Schiller Theater* Building in Chicago, a commission begun in the early months of 1891 and completed the following year.

Surviving drawings indicate the design Adler & Sullivan produced for the relatively inexpensive Stadt Theater project was based upon the prototype established at Pueblo, except the proscenium was to have been trumpet-shaped and the arcade around the main floor was omitted. For reasons of economy, columns had to be used to support the main balcony, and the ornamental treatment was intended to be rather sparse. Photographs of the executed work and the drawings show, however, that despite its small size, it would have been quite spacious and beautifully proportioned if executed as originally proposed.

Although the design for the exterior of the building at Seattle was not at all noteworthy, the interior would have been one of Adler's most remarkable. It was arranged much like the Stadt Theater, but whereas the Stadt revealed no particular geometric order, the principal features of this design were entirely circumscribed around a sphere.

The interior of the Schiller Theater was similar to the Stadt Theater, but far more ornate. The only significant differences were: the elaborate structural system of the Schiller eliminated the need for columns to support the balcony and gallery, and the ceiling in the forward part of the house was treated as a series of concentric full arches which radiated from the proscenium, not as a trumpet. The spandrels of these arches were faced with elaborate plaster grilles which served as continuous air supply vents that functioned in the same way as the vents in the vaulted ceiling of the Auditorium.

By plotting the passage of sound on a schematic longitudinal section of the Schiller Theater (fig. 2) as a series of straight lines from their average point of origin (a point five feet above the floor at the center of the stage), one can see the heavily ornamented surfaces of the radiating arches provide only diffused reflection in the forward part of the house (unlike the flat surface of the vaults of the Auditorium which provide some slight direct reflections back onto the main floor). The areas of smooth ceiling at the rear of the house remain near the lines of direct sound, so reflected sound could reinforce direct sound without creating an echo.

By the time Adler designed the Schiller, he had abandoned both the principle of promoting the free flow of air at the rear of the house and the extensive use of exposed light bulbs for ornamental effect. The foyers were, therefore, generally isolated from the house, and although the light bulbs remained exposed, they were more discreetly placed than in the Auditorium.

This was Adler's last theatre. In the eleven years after the Grand Opera House he departed radically from the accepted prototypes for theatre design. Despite his great knowledge of stage design, the stage of the Schiller, with its relatively narrow 29' proscenium, appears to have differed little from the

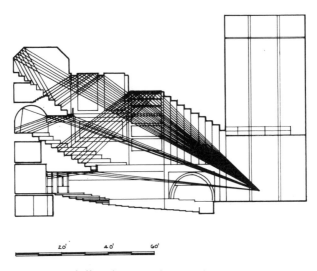

Fig. 2. Schiller Theater, schematic longitudinal section.

stages of the Grand Opera House and the Academy of Music (the earliest of his stages of which any substantial records exist), except a greater effort was made to make it fireproof.

Adler & Sullivan's commissions to design auditoriums were not limited to theatres. In addition to several convention halls, they also designed three Chicago synagogues: Zion Temple (1885), K.A.M. Temple (1890–91, now Pilgrim Baptist Church), and the rear addition and complete interior remodeling of the Burling & Adler Sinai Temple (1891–92). The interiors were basically alike. The seating was arranged according to Kinney's system. An effort was made to have as few obstructing columns as possible, and each had a high barrel-vaulted ceiling. In each, this latter feature resembled the ceilings used by August Bauer (Adler's first employer in Chicago) in his churches of the 1860s.[17] While this may show a belated influence of Bauer, this kind of ceiling is far more likely to produce diffused reflection of sound than the flat or slightly pitched ceilings used by Adler during his association with both the Kinneys and Burling. Although Adler had always endeavored to diminish the volume of his theatres, in these synagogues the high vaulted ceilings allowed the further advantage of sufficient reverberation for the organs housed in each.

In the Zion and Sinai temples, the barrel vault is nowhere evident on the exterior, but in the K.A.M. temple, its outer shell forms a large clerestory topped by a huge pyramided roof. This gives it a unique architectural character; it is one of few synagogues of the nineteenth century that does not look like a modified church or mosque.

The most prominent of Adler's executed works after the dissolution of his partnership with Sullivan was Isaiah Temple (now Ebenezer Baptist Church) in Chicago, which was designed in the early months of 1898 and dedicated roughly a year later. The internal arrangement of this building was similar to Adler's other synagogues, except the ceiling of the auditorium is a heavily coffered transverse barrel vault, a device apparently derived from the ceiling of the forward part of the theatre at Pueblo, Colorado. The exterior was similar to some of the more restrained work of Sir Christopher Wren. It is not known whether Adler was responsible for this. The design has no precedent in his earlier work, but several details, in particular the tracery of the windows, have their counterparts in the works of Adler & Sullivan.

One may wonder why, after writing widely on theatre design and executing such superb theatres, Adler's influence on the subsequent course of developments in the field has not been more pervasive. The reason seems tied to the fortunes of the reputation of his partner, Sullivan. Adler had so successfully promoted the reputation of his younger partner as a designer and decorator, that as Sullivan's national reputation declined following the rise of neoclassicism at the Columbian Exposition, so unfortunately did Adler's. At the time of his death he was no longer regarded as the senior partner in one of the nation's most innovative architectural firms, but only as a well-respected member of the local architectural community.

Today (more than ever before), architecture is judged by appearance rather than utility. Sullivan has been resurrected and transformed, not only as a "pioneer" but as "the prophet" of an architecture which he most assuredly would have rejected. He has been regarded as the primary, if not the sole, creator of those great works produced during his fifteen-year association with Dankmar Adler.[18] Adler invariably procured for the firm its most important commissions, and it was primarily he who determined their arrangement and structure. The general form of buildings like the Chicago Auditorium and the Schiller would have been much the same had Adler never known Sullivan. Had Sullivan not been Adler's partner, he would never have been involved with either project. The most just analysis of their roles in their greatest achievements would be that they were Adler's designs refined to brilliance by Sullivan.

1. *The Chicago Tribune*, March 2, 1879.

2. John Scott Russell: "Elementary Considerations of some Principles in the Construction of Buildings designed to accommodate Spectators and Auditors." *The Edinburgh New Philosophical Journal*, vol. XXVII, April–October 1839, pp. 131–136.

3. Dankmar Adler: "The Paramount Requirements of a Large Opera House," *The Inland Architect and News Record*, October 1887, p. 46.

4. Dankmar Adler: "Theater Building for American Cities," *The Engineering Magazine*, August 1894, p. 723.

5. Ibid., September, 1894, p. 815.

6. Adler discussed these principles at length in his papers, "Theater Building for American Cities" and "The Theatre" (see appendix).

7. "Theater Building for American Cities," August 1894, p. 724.

8. Ibid., September 1894, p. 816.

9. This had been accomplished in the Festspiel Haus at Bayreuth, erected in 1872–76, but only with one level of seating.

10. Dankmar Adler: "The Theatre," see appendix p. 208.

11. "The Paramount Requirements of a Large Opera House," p. 45.

12. Ibid., p. 46. This idea is also mentioned in James Fergusson: *History of the Modern Styles of Architecture*, vol. 2, book X, a popular history of the day that went through numerous editions and reprintings.

13. Ibid.

14. The records of the Auditorium Association, now in the Roosevelt University Archives, do not say why they were sent to Europe, but indicate that earlier in the year both Ferdinand Peck, president of the Association, and Milward Adams, then recently appointed manager of the theatre, had traveled to Europe to investigate stage equipment. Both had recommended use of the Asphalia equipment which Adler and Bairstow eventually secured.

15. Alfred Shaw: "Modern Opera Houses in Europe and America," in Arthur Waltersdorf, ed.: *Living Architecture* (Chicago, 1930) p. 52.

16. "Theater Building for American Cities," August 1894, pp. 729–730.

17. The Swedish Ev. Lutheran Immanuel Church erected in 1868 in Chicago was a typical example.

18. Hugh Morrison decided to call Sullivan "Prophet of Modern Architecture" as early as 1935. In his well known work, *Pioneers of Modern Design*, Nikolaus Pevsner erroneously refers at length to Sullivan alone as the designer of several of the more important Adler & Sullivan commissions.

CATALOG OF ADLER'S THEATRES AND AUDITORIUMS

1. Main Building
    College of Wooster
    Wooster, Ohio
    O.S. Kinney, Kinney & Adler
    1867–70
    No longer extant
    Seating capacity: Kauke Chapel: 800

The approved design for this Presbyterian institution was published in a lithograph copyrighted by O.S. Kinney in 1867. A copy, now in the possession of the College of Wooster, called for a mansarded five-story and basement central pavilion flanked at each side by identical mansarded four-story and basement wings with a total length of 305′ and a maximum width at the central pavilion of 130′ 8″. Only the central pavilion, dedicated on September 7, 1870, was actually constructed.

Because the chapel (called for in the original design) was to have been in one of the unbuilt wings, the lecture hall in the executed central pavilion (which Adler refers to in his autobiography) was redesignated at the time of construction as the Kauke Chapel. This chapel, which occupied the rear of the second and third floors, was a rectangular room 52′ × 56′ with a flat ceiling 28′ 6″ above the lowest point of its slightly sloped floor. A horseshoe balcony ran along the side and rear walls. The seating on the first floor was arranged in a curvilinear fashion.

The entire structure, by then augmented with wings similar to but smaller than those designed by Kinney, was destroyed by fire on December 11, 1901. Only its cornerstone (now set in a wall of the building which stands nearest to its site) survives.

Sources:

Douglas, Ben: *History of Wayne County Ohio*, 1878.
Notestein, Lucy Lilian: *Wooster of the Middle West*, 1937.
A large lithograph of O.S. Kinney's original design with a detailed description below.

2. First Methodist Episcopal Church
   Southeast corner of Rose and Lovell streets
   Kalamazoo, Michigan
   O.S. Kinney, Kinney & Adler
   1867–69
   No longer extant

This Romanesque building was designed in 1867 (prior to O.S. Kinney's death) but was not dedicated until September 12, 1869. It was 135′ long with an average width of 80′. The spire rose to a height of 170′.

Although no interior descriptions have been found, the great similarity of its exterior to the Second Presbyterian Church at La Porte, Indiana (catalog entry 4) suggests their interiors were also similar. The church was destroyed by fire on March 13, 1926.

Sources:

Durant, Samuel W.: *History of Kalamazoo County Michigan,* 1880.
The Inland Architect and News Record, May 1892.

3. Wilcoxon Opera House
   Northeast corner of Stephenson and Van Buren streets
   Freeport, Illinois
   Kinney & Adler
   1868–69
   No longer extant
   Seating capacity: 800 (main floor: 600, balcony: 200)

This four-story building had a frontage of 66′ along its south side and 77′ along its west side. Although the south front, which was constructed entirely of Joliet limestone (as opposed to the brick and stone used on the other front), was intended to be the principal elevation, the only elaborately treated portion of the facade was the pavilion created at the corner where they met, a feature found in other work done in the office of O.S. Kinney.

The design of the building appears to have been prepared in the fall of 1868, several months before Kinney's death. It was influenced by the decision of the building's owner, Thompson Wilcoxon, to incorporate portions of an existing three-story building, constructed on the site in 1854, into the new structure. The irregular fenestration of the west wall may have been related to the disposition of structural elements in the earlier building. The first floor was originally occupied by stores and a bank. The second floor contained offices that opened onto a 20′ × 40′ corridor which ran lengthwise along the center of the east party wall. Although this corridor could be reached by two staircases from entrances at either facade of the building, only the eastern one led to the auditorium above. The auditorium, 60′ × 50′, occupied the entire southern portion of the upper two floors. Although the balcony was raked, all sources (including an interview with a man who had been there) agreed that the main floor was level. The stage, 23′ deep and 45′ wide, was placed along the north wall. Adjoining it were four dressing rooms, a "large" property room, and a greenroom. The auditorium (if not the entire building) was heated by a gravity hot air furnace.

The theatre opened to the public on December 28, 1869. It remained one of the principal places of amusement in Freeport until the late 1890s, when competition from other halls made the Wilcoxon's third floor location unpopular. The auditorium was no longer in use by 1903 but remained intact until 1917, when it was gutted as part of a complete remodeling of the building in which a fifth floor was added, the facades were completely redone, and all floors above the first were converted to office use. On April 9, 1955, the building was destroyed by fire. The only portions of the original structure now visible are sections of the party walls. A one-story building now stands on the site.

Sources:

Anonymous: *Holland's Freeport City Directory 1872–73*, 1872.
Anonymous: *History of Stephenson County 1970*, 1970.
Tilden, M.H.: *The History of Stephenson County Illinois*, 1880.
The Freeport Journal, February 24, 1869; December 22, 1869; December 30, 1869; January 5, 1870.

4. Second Presbyterian Church
   (later The Presbyterian Church)
   Northeast corner of Main and Harrison streets
   La Porte, Indiana
   Kinney & Adler
   1869-71
   No longer extant
   Seating capacity: 680

Unlike the buildings previously described, this Romanesque church originated in the office of the firm of Kinney & Adler and was entirely the work of Dankmar Adler. It appears to have been designed in the spring of 1869 and was dedicated in July of 1871.

It was 102' long and 74' across the front. The height of the side walls was 40' from the foundation to the eaves. The front was to have been adorned by a 150' tower, never completed, but it was probably to have been identical to that of the Methodist Church in Kalamazoo (catalog entry 2). The first (or basement) floor had a clear ceiling height of 11' and was intended to be used mainly for a Sunday school. The auditorium on the second floor was 79' long by 58' wide. The ceiling was 28' above the floor at the sides and rose to a height of 40' along the center line of the room. The pews were arranged in straight lines.

The interior of the auditorium was remodeled several times without altering the ornamental truss work at the ceiling. It was similar in feeling to that of O.S. Kinney's (still extant) Presbyterian Church at Freeport, Illinois which was begun in 1866. In one of these remodelings, the main floor, originally level, was reconstructed with a slight rake. The last major remodeling, done in 1952, partially restored the room's nineteenth-century character, but in 1968 the entire building was demolished.

Sources:

Donaldson, John B.: *Historical Sketch and Diamond Jubilee of the Presbyterian Church, La Porte, Indiana*, 1908.
La Porte Argus, July 13, 1871.
The Union and Herald (La Porte), August 28, 1869.

5. Methodist Church Block
    Southeast corner of Washington and Clark streets
    Chicago, Illinois
    Burling & Adler
    1871–73
    No longer extant
    Seating capacity: 1,000

This is one of the few works of the firm of Burling & Adler that Adler claimed to have designed. It was begun shortly after the Chicago Fire of 1871 and was dedicated on November 2, 1873.

Its four-story Italianate stone facades had a frontage of 130′ on Clark Street and 80′ on Washington Street. In addition to the rooms used by the First Methodist Church in its upper floors, it had seven stores on the first floor and sixteen offices above. The auditorium, 65′ × 90′, occupied most of the third and fourth floor at the south end of the building. It had a horseshoe balcony with raked seating along its side and rear walls. Although the first floor was level, the seating was arranged in a curvilinear fashion. Behind the pulpit platform was an elaborate screen of organ pipes flanked on either side by a pair of Corinthian columns which supported a curved pediment and framed ornamental mottos. With its flat ceiling, it looked much like an enlarged version of the Kauke Chapel at Wooster, Ohio (catalog entry 1). It was lit by gas and heated by four stoves, one in each corner of the room.

The building remained in use, substantially as constructed, until it was demolished to make way for the present home of the congregation, The Chicago Temple, which was begun in 1922.

Sources:

Adler, Dankmar: Autobiography (manuscript).
Andreas, A.T.: *History of Chicago,* vol. 3, 1886.
Randall, Frank A.: *History of the Development of Building Construction in Chicago,* 1949.
The Chicago Tribune, April 20, 1873; November 3, 1873; November 23, 1873.
The Inter Ocean (Chicago), November 3, 1873.

6. Unity Church (now Scottish Rite Cathedral)
   Southeast corner of Dearborn and Walton streets
   Chicago, Illinois
   Burling & Adler
   1872–73
   Extant, interior heavily remodeled
   Seating capacity: 1,322 (main floor: 810, balcony: 512)

The cornerstone of this church, designed by Theodore V. Wadskier, was laid on August 29, 1867. The building was dedicated on June 20, 1869. After the Great Fire of 1871, Burling & Adler were commissioned to rebuild it within the surviving shell. Although Adler listed it in his autobiography among the works of the firm, without claiming authorship of the design, its great similarity to other churches designed by him and his former employer, O.S. Kinney, indicates that he exerted considerable influence in its design. The actual work of rebuilding the church began in March of 1872, and it was rededicated on December 7, 1873. While Burling & Adler's design featured two dissimilar towers, the existing towers are the work of other architects.

The building is 152′ long, 91′ across the front and 73′ wide at the auditorium. The height to the top of the roof is 85′ 6″. The first floor was originally devoted to a lecture room, kitchen, and other ancillary rooms. The auditorium, at the second floor level, is 70′ × 89′. Unlike Adler's earlier auditoriums, the plan of this was not rectangular but instead terminated at the east or pulpit end in a half octagon. Originally, the seating of the main floor was arranged in a curvilinear fashion. The seating on the main floor and in the balcony (which extended along the side and rear walls) was raked. These features are the first indications in Adler's work that he had begun to give serious consideration to the importance of proper acoustical design. The organ pipes appear to have been set originally behind an ornamental colonnade behind the pulpit and choir seats. If so, this would have been the first of several such installations to be found in Adler's work.

The church was sold to a Masonic lodge and renamed the Medinah Temple in 1902. The organ was then moved to the west end of the balcony, and a stage with rigging loft was erected in the space which it had occupied. The seating arrangement of the main floor was also changed at this time. The building was acquired by its present owners, The Scottish Rite Cathedral Association, in 1911.

Sources:

Adler, Dankmar: Autobiography (manuscript).
Andreas, A.T.: *History of Chicago*, vol. 2, 1885.
The Chicago Tribune, June 20, 1869; May 4, 1873; December 7, 1873.
The Chicago Evening Journal, December 6, 1873.

7. Kingsbury Music Hall
   New Chicago Theatre
   169 N. Clark Street
   Chicago, Illinois
   Burling & Adler
   1872–73, 1875
   No longer extant
   Seating capacity: 1,600

Although Adler mentioned (but did not take credit for the design of) the Kingsbury Music Hall in his autobiography, an article in *The Chicago Tribune* of March 2, 1879, attributes both its design and subsequent remodeling into the New Chicago Theatre entirely to him. This auditorium was actually located on the alley (Couch Place) at the rear of 66–72 W. Randolph Street. The address given above was only that of its corridor entrance, which throughout its history extended through the various buildings that adjoined it on the west. Before the Chicago Fire of 1871, another auditorium, known for a short time as Kingsbury Hall, occupied the site. Construction of the new hall began in 1872. Its opening on October 6, 1873 made it the first music hall to open in the central business district after the fire.

The auditorium was 80′ wide by 100′ long. The ceiling was 47′ above the main floor (at which end is not stated in the description), and at the apex of its ornate central skylight, it rose an additional 8′. The skylight was apparently required because the enclosed site prohibited the use of windows, such as Adler had used in all of his earlier auditoriums. The floor of the single horseshoe balcony rose from a height of 14′ 6″ at its lowest point to 20′ at its highest, and the main floor rose 6′ from front to back. The stage platform was 22′ deep by 50′ wide. The auditorium was basically an elongated octagon, which repeated the wall arrangement previously introduced for the pulpit end of the Unity Church (catalog entry 6) at both ends. Although this hall resembled its predecessors, the use of the skylight and of elaborate cove and beam work at the ceiling made it appear far more monumental.

The auditorium remained in use as a music hall for about one year, but according to A.T. Andreas in his *History of Chi-*

cago, it was too small for such use. When Adler remodeled it into the New Chicago Theatre (which opened on August 17, 1875), he added a new stage with rigging loft, 31′ deep and 83′ wide, and introduced a pair of boxes at either side of a new proscenium arch.

Although this theater had many other names, for most of its history it was known as the Olympic, and finally as the Apollo Theatre. In 1896, the theatre was again remodeled; a second balcony was added, and the proscenium reworked. The building survived until 1949, when it was demolished to make way for the bus terminal that now occupies the site.

Sources:

Adler, Dankmar: Autobiography (manuscript).
Andreas, A.T.: *History of Chicago*, vol. 3, 1886.
Randall, Frank A.: *History of the Development of Building Construction in Chicago*, 1949.
The Chicago Tribune, August 1, 1875; August 18, 1875; November 10, 1878; March 2, 1879; April 5, 1896.
The Inter Ocean (Chicago), August 30, 1896.
The Land Owner, October 1873.

8. First Congregational Church
   Northeast corner of Kenilworth Avenue and Lake Street
   Oak Park, Illinois
   Burling & Adler
   1873-74
   No longer extant
   Seating capacity: 525

This is another of the works of Burling & Adler for which Adler did not take credit in his autobiography. Its various High Victorian Gothic embellishments are identical to those found in known works of John H. Edelmann, then a Burling & Adler employee, and must be attributed to him. The general arrangement of the plan and the massing of the church are so similar to those of the works of O.S. Kinney and Kinney & Adler that one can assume Adler was responsible for these elements. Adler's deep involvement with this project might be further surmised from the fact that its chief sponsor, James W. Scoville, continued to patronize Adler long after the dissolution of his partnership with Burling. The design was produced in the early months of 1873. The cornerstone was laid on August 28, 1873, and the church was dedicated on November 1, 1874.

It was originally 80' long and 55' wide and had a tower 156' high. The auditorium was rectangular with a small alcove set behind the pulpit into which an organ, donated by Scoville in 1881, was later set. The seating on the main floor was arranged in a semi-circular fashion. The fact that the floor was level would have been of little significance in a so small a hall.

The church was considerably enlarged in 1892 and again in 1913 by additions constructed by other architects, but in 1916 the entire building was destroyed by fire. All that remains of the original structure are small portions of the walls, incorporated into the present church, which was constructed in 1918.

Sources:

Anonymous: *The First Congregational Church of Oak Park, Illinois, A Souvenir of the Thirty-Eighth Anniversary of Its Organization*, 1901.

Adler, Dankmar: Autobiography (manuscript).

Platt, Frank J.: *Century of Promise*, 1963.

The Chicago Tribune, April 20, 1873; November 1, 1874.

9. Sinai Temple
    Southwest corner of Indiana Avenue and 21st Street
    Chicago, Illinois
    Burling & Adler, Adler & Sullivan
    1875–76, 1884, 1891–92
    No longer extant
    Seating capacity: 1,080 (main floor: 930, balcony: 150)
    in 1876

Burling & Adler were awarded this project on February 8, 1875, after a limited competition against four other Chicago architectural firms. Although Adler claimed sole responsibility for this design in his autobiography, many of its High Victorian embellishments were designed by John H. Edelmann, who was then a partner in the firm of Johnston & Edelmann, and by their employee Louis H. Sullivan. Construction began on May 1, 1875, and the synagogue was dedicated on April 8, 1876.

The building was originally 92' wide and 130' long. The side walls were 52' high, and the walls of the central tower at the front were 90' high with a square dome above which extended to a height of 150'. The first floor was occupied by Sabbath school rooms. The auditorium on the second floor was 84' wide and 115' long, and it terminated in a half octagon at the pulpit platform end. The ceiling, which appears to have been ornamented with wood truss work like that which Adler had used in his earlier churches, rose to a height of 52'. The large organ was located in a gallery above and behind the pulpit platform which projected somewhat over the latter to form a sounding board. The main floor was again arranged in a semi-circular fashion with a rise of 2½'. A gallery extended in a straight line across the rear of the room. In 1884, the firm of Adler & Sullivan designed side galleries for the auditorium.

In the spring of 1891, Adler & Sullivan were retained to undertake an extensive remodeling of the building. This work, which was completed for the rededication of the synagogue on September 22, 1892, involved demolition of a substantial portion of the rear of the original building, construction of an addition that extended the building to the rear of the property, and extensive changes to the interior of the auditorium, which in the process was also lengthened. While every effort was made to make the new addition blend well with the exterior of the older building, few signs of the original work were left when the interior remodeling was completed. The truss work at the ceiling was replaced by a barrel vault, and the pulpit platform and organ, although still related in the same manner, featured an elaborate two-story arcaded screen.

The congregation remained in this building until 1912, when a new synagogue was constructed at another location. The old building was subsequently demolished.

Sources:

Adler, Dankmar: Autobiography (manuscript).
Strauss, Irma: *Adler & Sullivan and the Sinai Temple* (University of Chicago graduate paper), 1974.
The Chicago Times, April 9, 1876; May 21, 1876.
The Chicago Tribune, April 8, 1876.
The Reform Advocate, September 30, 1892.
Western Electrician, December 15, 1894.

10. Central Music Hall
    Southeast corner of State and Randolph streets
    Chicago, Illinois
    Burling & Adler, Dankmar Adler, D. Adler & Co.,
    Adler & Sullivan
    1878–80, 1883, 1890
    No longer extant
    Seating capacity: Music Hall: 1,785
    (main floor: 800, balcony: 540, gallery: 445);
    Fairbanks Hall: 500; Apollo Hall: 400

Not long after the founding of Rev. David Swing's Central Church on December 4, 1875, George B. Carpenter, a local promoter of concerts and lectures and member of the church, conceived the idea of a building to be named in its honor that would provide a home for the church, and also feature a concert hall, stores, and offices. Carpenter did not have to look far to find the financial resources that would be needed to make his idea a reality. Among Rev. Swing's followers were a number of Chicago's wealthiest businessmen including Ferdinand W. Peck, N.K. Fairbanks, and George Pullman. With their support, Carpenter established a stock company to purchase the land and construct the building. He expected, and was ultimately given, a large share of the company's stock as a reward for his participation.

In an interview in *The Chicago Times* of March 2, 1879, Carpenter stated that he had worked with Adler from the project's inception and together they had developed six different designs including that from which the building was being constructed. During this design process, Adler came upon (probably with Carpenter's help) most of the principles of good acoustical design that were to eventually give him a national reputation in the field. Although most sources credit the firm of D. Adler, Architect as the source of the design, an article in *The Chicago Tribune* of December 25, 1878, clearly shows that the drawings had been substantially completed while Burling was still Adler's partner. The remarkable similarity between the basically Italianate facades of this bulding and those of the First National Bank in Chicago, designed by former Burling & Adler employee Francis M. Whitehouse two years later, suggests that Whitehouse, like Edelmann before him, was responsible for the architectural embellishment of this Adler design.

The building had a frontage of 124' on State Street and 150' 6" on Randolph Street. The main auditorium occupied the entire east half of the site, the remainder of which was filled by the six-story office section with a small light court at its southeast corner. This section originally contained six stores on the first floor; seventy offices and studios in the floors above; Fairbanks Hall, a recital hall in the southwest corner of the fourth and fifth floors, and the rehearsal rooms of the Apollo Club in the same area on the sixth floor. The main auditorium occupied a rectangular space 124' × 86'. Internally the corners of the end opposite the street were cut off by the chambers for the organ pipes, which gave the hall the same kind of half octagon stage end found in several of Adler's earlier auditoriums. Between the organ cases at the second floor level was an arcaded gallery which held the console of the organ and served as an ornamental backdrop for the stage platform. Both the organ cases and this gallery were designed by Louis Sullivan and were installed roughly a year after the hall opened. Two horseshoe balconies with boxes at the ends closest to the organ cases, and supported on cast iron columns, ran along the sides and rear of the hall. All seating was arranged in a curvilinear fashion with a steep rise which followed the *isacoustic curve*. The ceiling featured elaborate cove and beam work with a stained glass skylight at the center, all similar to those used in the Kingsbury Music Hall (catalog entry 7). The chorus rooms, dressing rooms, check rooms, and toilet rooms were all located in the basement under the main floor seating.

Construction began in the spring of 1879, and on December 5th of that year, the somewhat unfinished main auditorium was opened to the public. In 1883, Fairbanks Hall was gutted and the space turned into thirteen offices under the direction of D. Adler & Co. In 1890, the rooms of the Apollo Club including Apollo Hall were extensively remodeled by Adler & Sullivan.

In 1901, the entire building was demolished to make way for the retail store of Marshall Field and Company which still occupies the site. One of the columns from the State Street entrance was preserved and later placed over Adler's grave in Mount Mayriv Cemetery in Chicago.

Sources:

Adler, Dankmar: Autobiography (manuscript).
The Chicago Daily News, December 4, 1879.
The Chicago Times, March 2, 1879; December 4, 1879; February 6, 1880; May 8, 1883.
The Chicago Tribune, December 24, 1878; March 2, 1879; December 5, 1879; February 6, 1880; October 22, 1880; September 21, 1890.
The Inter Ocean (Chicago), December 24, 1878; December 5, 1879; February 6, 1880.

11. Grand Opera House
    119–21 North Clark Street
    Chicago, Illinois
    Dankmar Adler
    1880
    No longer extant
    Seating capacity: 1,750

In January of 1872, the site of this building was acquired by brothers John A. and Lycander B. Hamlin. Shortly thereafter, they constructed a four-story store and office building at the front of the property. In 1873, they erected an addition to the rear of this building which was initially used as a billiard hall. After several changes in use and the construction of at least one more addition, the rear of the building was again remodeled in 1878 to become Hamlin's Theatre.

In the latter part of 1879, the property was acquired by John Borden, who gave it to his son William. One of them subsequently commissioned Adler to remodel all but the upper floors of the front portion of the building. Although only the entrance corridors on the first floor were reworked in the original part of the building, the entire rear was rebuilt, leaving only portions of the old north and rear walls intact. A permit was issued for the work on May 7, 1880, and on September 6, 1880, the theatre was reopened as the Grand Opera House.

The irregularly shaped auditorium had a maximum depth of 80′ 6″ and a maximum width of 77′ 8″. The seating throughout the auditorium was arranged in a curvilinear fashion with rises determined by the *isacoustic curve* principle. The proscenium opening was 32′ square and was flanked at either side by two levels of ornate proscenium boxes with two boxes at each level. The main balcony and gallery above were supported at their fronts by cast iron columns and followed the truncated horseshoe pattern that was then typical of most American theatres. Although the surface of the ceiling was broken up with heavy beams, the elaborate coving that had been a feature of Adler's concert halls was omitted in favor of sloped segments of flat ceiling. As the ceiling approached the stage, it became progressively lower until it met the top of the proscenium opening.

The stage house was 77′ 8″ wide by roughly 37′ deep and was 56′ high from the stage floor to the rigging loft. Although the walls of the stage house were of load bearing masonry, the remainder of the construction was of wood.

The internal decoration of the building appears to have been the first task given Louis Sullivan after he entered Adler's office. While the interiors of Adler's earlier auditoriums (with the exception of the Sinai Temple, which was also decorated by Sullivan) had relatively restrained color schemes, on this building he used a multitude of garish colors that ranged from green and maroon to blue and black.

In 1899, during remodeling done under the direction of architect George A. Garnsey, two floors were added to the front of the building, and some alterations were made to the auditorium. In a remodeling directed by architect Andrew Rebori in 1927, the entire facade and interior of the auditorium were completely reconstructed. The building remained unchanged until it was demolished to make way for the building then known as the Chicago Civic Center.

Sources:

Andreas, A.T.: *History of Chicago*, vol. 3, 1886.
Randall, Frank A.: *History of the Development of Building Construction in Chicago*, 1949.
Waltersdorf, Arthur: *Living Architecture*, 1930.
The Chicago Journal, September 4, 1880.
The Chicago Times, September 5, 1880.
The Inter Ocean (Chicago), September 7, 1880.
The Chicago Tribune, August 29, 1880; September 5, 1880.

12. Academy of Music
    131 South Rose Street
    Kalamazoo, Michigan
    Dankmar Adler
    1881–82
    No longer extant
    Seating capacity: 1,250 (main floor and balcony: 800, gallery: 450)

For a number of years, the citizens of Kalamazoo had desired a first class theatre, but because of the speculative nature of such a venture, none of them wanted to become its sole backer. Since some inducement was needed to attract sufficient capital, the citizens subscribed to a fund payable to anyone who would purchase a site and erect a theatre of appropriate size and cost. This offer led to the formation of the Kalamazoo Opera House Company and the purchase of the above site in the spring of 1881.

On June 3, 1881, Frederick Bush and L.B. Kendall, two of the company's directors, went to Chicago to procure plans and specifications for the new building. They were so impressed by Adler's work in the Central Music Hall and Grand Opera House that they soon selected him as the architect. This was the only theatre commission that Adler undertook before the Chicago Auditorium not, in some way, built around earlier construction.

The building was 67′ wide and 158′ deep. It was constructed of masonry bearing walls with timber framing and cast iron columns and was divided into three sections. At the front of the property stood a three-story office and store building, 40′ deep, with an 80′ tower marking the main entrance. Behind, the auditorium occupied the full width of the property and had a length of approximately 80′. Sullivan's elaborate ornamental treatment of both the exterior and interior of these portions of the building bore a great resemblance to that of S.S. Beman's Arcade Building at Pullman, Illinois, designed a year earlier. Behind the auditorium at the rear of the lot was the stage which was also the full width of the property and 38′ deep. From the floor to the rigging loft, it was 56′ high.

The only irregularities in the auditorium's basically rectangular plan resulted from the presence of a pair of two-tiered boxes at each side of the proscenium which was 30' wide and 32' high. The seating throughout the auditorium was arranged in a curvilinear fashion with a truncated horseshoe-shaped main balcony and gallery above, all supported on cast iron columns. As in its immediate predecessor, the Grand Opera House, the ceiling became progressively lower as it approached the proscenium, but instead of sloped panels throughout, only the portion of the ceiling which adjoined the proscenium was so treated. The remainder of the ceiling was made up of three level panels divided by ornamental beams and connected to each other and the outer walls by heavy coves like those used in the Central Music Hall. The auditorium was lit by over 400 gas jets; during the day, light could be obtained through two large windows at either side of the auditorium.

The theatre portion of the building was heated by an elaborate steam-operated gravity hot air system. Cold air was drawn into the basement where it was warmed by banks of steam pipes. From there it rose through vents in the floor and was exhausted through vents in the roof and in the foyer and galleries by ductwork to two ventilation shafts, one at one side of the stage and the other at the rear of the auditorium at the opposite side of the building. Heat induced by a steam coil in the shaft in the auditorium and by the smoke flue of the main chimney in the shaft at the stage then expelled the exhaust air above the roof.

From the beginning and throughout most of its history, the theatre was under the management of Benjamin A. Bush, who eventually acquired full ownership of the property from Bush and Patterson, the general contractors who built it and had acquired the shares of the Kalamazoo Opera House Company upon its completion. The property remained in the hands of the estate of Benjamin Bush until 1945. Until its destruction by arson on June 10, 1930, the auditorium served as a legitimate theatre, except for a brief period when it was known as "The Regent" and served as a movie house. Although the fire completely destroyed the auditorium, the three-story office portion, shorn of its cornice and tower roof, remained until 1967, when it was demolished to make way for the Industrial State Bank, which now occupies the site.

Sources:

Anonymous: *Portraits and Biographical Record of Kalamazoo, Allegan and Van Buren Counties, Michigan*, 1892.
Gregersen, Charles E.: "Early Adler & Sullivan Work in Kalamazoo," *The Prairie School Review*, Third Quarter, 1974.
Kalamazoo Daily Telegraph, May 7, 1882.
Kalamazoo Weekly Telegraph, May 10, 1882.
Kalamazoo Gazette, October 3, 1948; November 12, 1967.

13. First May Festival Hall (1882)

14. Second May Festival Hall—
     Republican and Democratic National
     Convention halls (1884)
     Interstate Industrial Exposition Building
     East side of Michigan Avenue between
     Monroe and Jackson streets
     Chicago, Illinois
     D. Adler & Co. (13), Adler & Sullivan (14)
     No longer extant
     Seating capacity: 9,180 (14)

These apparently similar auditoriums were temporary remodelings of the great central hall of the Interstate Industrial
Exposition Building, an extremely long room with rounded
ends, whose roof was supported by semicircular wood arches
with a clear span of 150'. The Exposition Building was a huge
structure 800' long and 260' wide, designed by architect
W.W. Boyington in 1873. Only two facts about the first of these
halls survive: it had a large sounding board over the stage platform at the south end of the room, and access to the aisles was
through tunnels painted in colors to match the tickets (so
members of the audience could easily locate their seats). In
addition to these features, the second hall occupied only 400'
of the central hall's length, and a second sounding board was
placed over the end of the room opposite the stage.
    At the conclusion of the festivals, which lasted only a few
days, these structures were dismantled. The Exposition Building was demolished in 1891 to make way for the Art Institute
Building which still occupies the site.

Sources:

Anonymous: *The Inter-State Exposition Souvenir*, Chicago,
    1873.
Andreas, A.T.: *History of Chicago*, vol. 3, 1886.
The Chicago Herald, June 1, 1884.
The Chicago Tribune, May 14, 21 and 28, 1882; May 31, 1884;
    June 1, 1884.
The Inland Architect and News Record, June 1884.

15. Hooley's Theatre (interior remodeling)
    124 West Randolph Street
    Chicago, Illinois
    D. Adler & Co.
    1882
    No longer extant
    Seating capacity: 1,506

The remodeling work done by D. Adler & Co. on this theatre was primarily cosmetic. The only significant changes were made in the proscenium and adjoining boxes. To overcome certain sight line and structural problems which had been peculiar to this theatre since its construction in 1872, Adler arranged three tiers of paired boxes on elaborate cast iron frames at either side of the proscenium. He was probably not satisfied with this solution which, although it must have been an improvement, could only have been partially successful. In any event, he never used it again.

In the extensive remodeling of the auditorium by architects Wilson and Marshall in 1898, most of this work was destroyed but the original shape of the galleries was maintained. It was then renamed Powers Theatre. It was demolished to make way for an addition to the Sherman House, erected in 1925, which in turn was demolished to make way for an office building for the State of Illinois.

Sources:

Flinn, John J.: *The Standard Guide to Chicago*, 1893.
Randall, Frank A.: *History of the Development of Building Construction in Chicago*, 1949.
The Chicago Evening Journal, August 12, 1882.
The Chicago Herald, August 13, 1882.
The Chicago Times, August 13, 1882.
The Chicago Tribune, August 13, 1882.
The Daily Inter Ocean (Chicago), August 13, 1882.

16. McVicker's Theatre (remodeling and addition)
    25 West Madison Street
    Chicago, Illinois
    Adler & Sullivan
    1883–85, 1890–91
    Only partially extant
    Seating capacity: 1,865

In the spring of 1883, Adler & Sullivan were commissioned to prepare drawings for the complete renovation of this theatre which had been erected in 1872 to the designs of architects Otis Wheelock and Cyrus P. Thomas. The project was delayed for some time, and the remodeled theatre did not open until July 1, 1885.

This remodeling involved the addition of two floors of offices to the top of the front of the building (which brought its height to six stories), reconstruction of the ceiling and proscenium of the auditorium, redecoration of the remainder of the theatre (including the entrances), and installation of new heating and electrical lighting systems. Adler raised the ceiling at the rear of the gallery and made it progressively lower as it approached the proscenium as he had done in the theatres which immediately preceded this. The configuration and location of the original horseshoe balcony and gallery were not changed in this remodeling. The heating system was basically similar to that used in the Academy of Music at Kalamazoo (catalog entry 12), but instead of moving the air by convection, fans were used, and the direction of the movement of air within the auditorium was reversed (introduced at the ceiling and exhausted at the floor). A separate four-story building was erected across the alley to house the boilers. The novel use of bare electric light bulbs in ornamental plaster settings to illuminate the theatre appears to have been the first use of such a system of illumination.

On the morning of August 19, 1890, a fire started under the stage and destroyed it, the proscenium, the boxes, the entire roof of the auditorium, and part of the top gallery, but left the office portion intact, and the remainder of the theatre partially damaged by water. Not long after the fire, Adler & Sullivan were again commissioned to rebuild the theatre, which reopened on March 30, 1891. The work undertaken in this second remodeling was almost as extensive as that in the first. The interior of the auditorium was completely redecorated. The upper tier of proscenium boxes was eliminated, which reduced their number from twelve to six. The configuration of the balcony and gallery remained the same, but rather than rebuild the roof in its earlier form, Adler added two floors of offices above the auditorium which were carried on massive steel trusses spanning its width. The building's general arrangement otherwise remained substantially as it was after completion of the first remodeling, and no changes were made in the front office section, including the theatre's entrance.

Despite several further alterations to the front and foyer, the remodeled building remained intact until 1922. In that year, everything except portions of the rear and side walls, erected in 1872, was removed to make way for a new theatre of the same name. Primarily used as a movie house, it was demolished in the 1970s. The building at the rear of 20–22 South State Street, constructed as the boiler house in 1885, is all that remains of Adler & Sullivan's work.

Sources:

Randall, Frank A.: *History of the Development of Building Construction in Chicago*, 1949.

The American Architect and Building News, December 24, 1887; February 11, 1888.

The Chicago Times, July 1, 1885.

The Chicago Tribune, August 27, 1890; March 22, 1891.

The Evening News (Chicago), November 22, 1890.

The Inland Architect and News Record, September 1884; January 1885; May 1885.

The Inter Ocean (Chicago), June 21, 1885; July 2, 1885; March 31, 1891.

17. Haverly's Theatre (entrance remodeling)
57 West Monroe Street
Chicago, Illinois
Adler & Sullivan
1884
No longer extant

This theatre was erected in 1881 to the designs of architect Oscar Cobb. In 1884, Adler & Sullivan were commissioned to remodel the entrances. Two stores at either side of the central entrance were converted to art galleries and foyer space, and additional dressing rooms and scene storage was constructed at the rear of the property adjoining the stage. This work was completed by September of that year.

The theatre's name was changed to the Columbia Theatre in 1885. On March 30, 1900, the building was completely destroyed by fire. Shortly thereafter, the Inter Ocean Building, now demolished, was constructed on the site.

Sources:

Andreas, A.T.: *History of Chicago*, vol. 3, 1886.
Gilbert, Paul and Charles Lee Bryson: *Chicago and Its Makers*, 1929.
The Inland Architect and News Record, July 1884; September 1884.

18. Opera Festival Hall
    Interstate Industrial Exposition Building
    East side of Michigan Avenue between
    Monroe and Jackson streets
    Chicago, Illinois
    Adler & Sullivan
    1885
    No longer extant
    Seating capacity: 6,200 (parquet: 2,238,
    dress circle: 1,486, side balconies: 352,
    main balcony: 1,824, boxes: 300)

The idea of an "opera festival" in the Exposition Building was first proposed by Silas G. Pratt in February of 1882 at a meeting with the renowned impresario, Col. J.H. Mapleson. However, it was not until April 14, 1884, through Pratt's initiative, that the Chicago Opera Festival Association was chartered with Ferdinand W. Peck as its president.

Adler's friendship with a number of the Festival Association's directors and his successful remodeling of the Exposition Building for the May Festivals of 1882 and 1884, (catalog entries 13–14) led to Adler & Sullivan's commission to design the auditorium on January 17, 1885. Construction began less than a month later, and by March 28, 1885, the auditorium was complete with the exception of the installation of the draperies and gas lighting fixtures.

The auditorium occupied the full 150′ width of the central hall of the Exposition Building and extended 196′ 10″ back from the proscenium to the rear of the last row of seats on the main floor. While the seating on the main floor was arranged around a common center point at the rear of the stage, all the seating in the main balcony at the rear of the auditorium was arranged in a straight line for reasons of economy. At either side of the 60′ × 40′ proscenium were two levels of boxes, which totaled sixty in all, with an ornately painted sounding board above. In order to take advantage of this sounding board, the stage floor was extended 19′ past the proscenium into the house. Additional seating was provided by a small gallery at each side of the auditorium between the boxes and main balcony.

The stage and dressing and storage rooms filled the entire north end of the Exposition Building. Its 80′ depth and 127′ width, with the rigging loft at 61′ above the stage floor, was the largest Adler ever designed, but it was built entirely of wood.

After the festival's twelve-day run, the auditorium was used by several other opera companies. It was then dismantled to make way for the industrial exposition of that year.

Sources:

Andreas, A.T.: *History of Chicago*, vol. 3, 1886.
Pratt, S.G.: *First Chicago Grand Opera Festival*, 1885.
The Chicago Tribune, March 1, 1885.
The Inland Architect and News Record, February 1885; March 1885.

19. Zion Temple
    East side of Ogden Avenue immediately south of
    Washington Boulevard
    Chicago, Illinois
    Adler & Sullivan
    1885
    No longer extant
    Seating capacity: approximately 1,000

Adler & Sullivan undoubtedly received this commission because of Adler's prominence in the Jewish community. Construction began on May 1, 1885, and the completed building was dedicated on September 5, 1885.

It was 65' across the front and 115' long. Although the original design of the front with its twin onion-domed towers would have made the building somewhat monumental, the omission of these features in the completed building gave it a stumpy appearance that Sullivan's crude Moorish-inspired details only accentuated. The first floor of the building was occupied by Sabbath school rooms. The auditorium on the second floor was 60' wide, roughly 100' long, and had a high trefoil barrel vaulted ceiling. The plan terminated in a half octagon at the end opposite the entrance where the pulpit platform was located. At the rear of this platform, somewhat squashed under a segmental arch, stood the ark, a feature of traditional synagogue architecture that was here treated as an elaborate onion-domed baldachino. Although surviving documentation is unclear, it is known that the seating on the main floor had a slight rise and most likely followed a curvilinear plan. Additional seating was provided by a gallery that extended along the sides of the room and across the rear, where it also housed a large organ. In order to insure that all the seats on the main floor would have an unobstructed view of the ark and its platform, heavy cantilevered brackets were used to support the side galleries.

The building remained in use as a synagogue with only minor alterations until about 1920, when the congregation merged with another and moved to Oak Park, Illinois. It was then sold to a labor union. In 1930, it was seriously damaged by fire but was subsequently rebuilt in a greatly altered form.

It remained until the early 1950s, when it was demolished to make way for the union building that now stands on the site.

Sources:

Schick, L.: *Chicago and Its Environs*, 1891.
The American Israelite, September 18, 1885.
The Chicago Daily News, September 5, 1885.
The Chicago Herald, September 5, 1885.
The Inland Architect and News Record, June 1885; September 1885.
The Inter Ocean (Chicago), September 5, 1885.

20. North American Saengerfest Hall
   Milwaukee Industrial Exposition Building
   Block bounded by Kilbourn, State, Fifth and Sixth streets
   Milwaukee, Wisconsin
   Adler & Sullivan
   1885–86
   No longer extant
   Seating capacity: 10,002 (main floor: 7,502,
   galleries: 2,500)

The Milwaukee Industrial Exposition Building was designed by architect E. Townsend Mix and constructed in 1881. It was 400′ long and 290′ wide. The height of the main roof was 89′ above grade and that of the dome was 150′.

Adler was apparently commissioned to remodel the interior in the fall of 1885 by the Milwaukee Musical Society for a "Saengerfest" to be held in the spring of the following year. This remodeling was similar to those he had already done for the May Festivals of 1882 and 1884 in Chicago (catalog entry 13–14). A sounding board was placed over the stage, which was raked for the chorus. Raked seating of ordinary wood chairs was provided on the main floor and in the galleries. The room was illuminated by electric arc lights.

The "Saengerfest" ran from July 21–25, 1886. At its conclusion, the auditorium arrangements were dismantled. The Exposition Building was destroyed by fire on June 4, 1905. The Milwaukee Auditorium, completed in 1909, now occupies the site.

Sources:

Gregory, John G.: *History of Milwaukee, Wisconsin*, vol. 1, 1931.
Saltzstein, Joan W.: "Saengerfest to Skat-Expo '81," *Milwaukee*, December 1966.
Harper's Weekly, July 31, 1886.
The Inland Architect and News Record, December 1885; August 1886.

21. Chicago Auditorium
    North side of Congress Street from
    Michigan to Wabash avenues
    Chicago, Illinois
    Adler & Sullivan
    1886–90
    Extant
    Seating capacity: 4,237 (main floor: 1,442,
    balcony: 1,632, lower gallery: 526,
    upper gallery: 437, boxes: 200)

The success of the Opera Festival of 1885 (catalog entry 18)
convinced Ferdinand W. Peck and his associates in that enterprise that Chicago needed a large permanent hall for operatic,
choral, and orchestral performances. They had originally proposed to construct the hall as a publicly funded institution,
but because of public controversy, they concluded at the end
of that year it could only be built as a private enterprise.

Because the high vacancy rates that were inherent in the
operation of halls of this size had always prevented them from
being self-supporting, Peck and his associates realized that it
would be necessary to construct some kind of large commercial edifice in conjunction with the hall. The proposed structure would require a very large site, but none was available in
the central business district. The only site with any potential
was along the Lakefront in an area then occupied primarily by
hotels, private residences, and some store and factory buildings. Peck and his associates would have preferred the auxiliary edifice be an office building (because of the comparative
ease of managing such a structure), but at this location only
a hotel seemed likely to succeed. They decided at least a small
part of the building would be devoted to offices, in the hope
that the great hall would eventually attract office tenants. By
July of 1886, with the entire site under their control, they obtained a charter to establish the Chicago Grand Auditorium
Association ("Grand" was dropped early the following year)
to own, construct, and manage the building and to lease the
land upon which it would stand.

Although Adler's firm was still small and relatively insignifi-
cant, Peck's confidence in Adler's ability to design an acousti-

cally superior hall convinced him that Adler & Sullivan should design the building. They began preliminary plans for the building in the spring of 1886 with no commitment other than Peck's personal assurance that they would be selected as the architects.

The earliest design of which any record exists was not prepared until September of 1886. It called for a stone and brick structure carried on a cast iron and steel frame (such as William Le Baron Jenney had used a year earlier in the Home Insurance Building) with ornate turrets, gables, and oriels. Although this was the first design prepared for the entire site as eventually acquired, the disposition of its various elements indicated that the final arrangement of its internal functions (with certain minor exceptions) already had been determined. This called for a hotel on the south and east fronts and an office building on the west, all surrounding the theatre at the rear, which was to be reached through an entrance at the base of a tall tower. The disposition of these various elements was determined by Adler entirely on the basis of real estate market conditions, light and ventilation requirements, and the configuration of the site. The result was the office portion fronted on Wabash Avenue, then a commercial street, and the hotel fronted on both Michigan Avenue and Congress Street, then primarily residential. The theatre, where natural light and ventilation would only have been a nuisance, was accordingly placed at the rear. The tower, which contained the tanks for the hydraulic elevator equipment, was placed on the Congress Street side to mark the entrance to the theatre and provide a visual (if not always functional) separation between the hotel and office sections.

By December, the project had progressed enough for the association to elect a board of directors, and on December 22, the newly elected board finally confirmed the appointment of Adler & Sullivan as architects, despite the objections of several board members, who would have preferred to give the commission to the then far more prominent firm of Burnham and Root. For the next three years, both Adler and Sullivan devoted most of their time to the largest structure of their careers.

After further complete revisions of the design, much of the

cast iron framing was eliminated in favor of load bearing masonry, and all the relief ornament, gables, turrets, and oriels were removed. As construction began, in March of 1887, a fourth design had been developed that was slightly higher than the original but still primarily of brick; it looks much like the completed building. Three more revisions, in which the brick was eliminated in favor of limestone and the height of the tower was further increased, were made before the building was completed. It was this slow process of revisions, rather than a conscious effort on the part of Adler & Sullivan, that caused the completed building to resemble Richardson's Marshall Field Warehouse.

At its completion in 1890, the Chicago Auditorium was the largest public building in America. It has a frontage, above its battered base, of 172' on the east or Michigan Avenue side (not including the portion over the alley which extends the frontage 16' 1¾" further north); 360' 10" on the south or Congress Street side, and 161' on the west or Wabash Avenue side. In general the facades are ten stories or 144' from the original grade line to the top of the coping. At the tower, which has a frontage of 76' 10" on the Congress Street elevation and a depth of 40' 4", it rose another seven (now eight due to the recent division of one of the floors into two) stories above the rest of the building to a height of 240' 2" at the top of the coping. Originally a two-story belvedere used by the Weather Bureau stood above the roof of the tower. (For further details of the evolution of the building's design, see pages 16 through 23 and Adler's own description, which begins on page 175 in the appendix.)

In spite of its tremendous importance to Chicago's cultural life and the great sum spent on its construction (slightly over $3,000,000), the building was never a financial success. Circulation problems that resulted because the hotel's 400 guest rooms had to be wrapped around the body of the auditorium forever required portions of it to be over-staffed. These problems were further aggravated by the hotel's disproportionately large public facilities. The restaurant facilities, for example, included a banquet hall on the seventh floor, a huge dining hall on the tenth floor, and a bar and restaurant on the first floor. While these all might normally have been serviced by one kitchen, their locations at opposite ends of the building required the construction of two separate kitchens.

The hotel and office building, however, did continue over the years to produce a profit sufficient to pay the taxes and the interest on the bonds which the Auditorium Association had been forced to issue in order to complete the building. The only dividend the stockholders ever received was for the year 1893, when visitors to the Columbian Exposition jammed the hotel. After almost forty years as the exclusive home of grand opera in Chicago, the Auditorium had become one of the city's most venerable institutions, but nothing could save the Auditorium Association from receivership when the first of its bond issues came due on February 1, 1929. To make matters worse, the Chicago Civic Opera Company, which at the time was the building's most important tenant, had a month earlier left for new quarters out of fear that the Association's imminent collapse would adversely affect its own operation. With all available funds exhausted, the receiver returned the building to the land owners in accordance with the terms of the original leases in 1932.

In 1932 and 1933, hoping to take advantage of the tourist trade created by the Century of Progress Exposition, the Auditorium Building Corporation, which had been formed to represent the interests of all but one of the owners in the operation of the building, undertook a major renovation. No amount of revitalization could overcome the effects of the Great Depression, which further reduced the Auditorium's already meager income. By 1941, the Auditorium Building Corporation, which owed roughly $1,150,000 in back taxes and penalties, decided to close the building. The failure of the Auditorium as a private enterprise was complete.

Despite all their efforts, neither the county nor city was able to acquire full ownership of the building through tax foreclosure proceedings, because the taxes on one part of the property, which belonged to an owner who had not been part of the Auditorium Building Corporation, had been paid in full. The city eventually acquired a tax title to the other properties, and by September of 1942, it had taken over part of the building for use as a City Service Men's Center. Unfortunately, during this period much of the ornament in the hotel portion was disfigured by over painting, and the bar, one of the building's most famous architectural features, was destroyed to make way for a lunch counter. The Service Men's Center remained in the building for a short period after the end of World War II, but by February of 1947, the newly organized Roosevelt University had managed to acquired title to the property from all of the former land owners. Although the university had full control of the building, the matter of the unpaid taxes still had to be settled. In 1952, in exchange for an easement which allowed the City of Chicago to cut an "arcade" through the first floor of the Congress Street side for the widening of the street, the taxes were waived. Unfortunately, in constructing the arcade, the former restaurant and the remainder of the bar were destroyed.

In 1957, the university undertook its first major restoration project with the partial restoration of the former banquet hall over the theatre as the Rudolf Ganz Recital Hall. In 1960, the university established the Auditorium Theatre Council to undertake the restoration of the theatre. Seven years later, the partially restored theatre again opened to the public, after over a quarter century. Since that time, the Theatre Council has continued the restoration work and made necessary improvements to the stage and dressing rooms. As funds become available, restoration work continues in other parts of the building.

It would be wrong to assume that because the Auditorium failed as a private enterprise that the building was a failure. Ferdinand Peck and the other wealthy patrons of the arts never expected it to make a profit. They knew they were taking a gamble, but when it was completed they got what they paid for—the finest opera house in America (if not the world)—nothing more, but nothing less.

Sources:

Adler, Dankmar: "The Chicago Auditorium," *Architectural Record*, April–June 1892.
Garczynski, Edward R.: *Auditorium*, 1890.

Gregersen, Charles E.: *The Chicago Auditorium, A History and Description* (manuscript prepared for publication by the Historic American Building Survey), 1980.

Moore, Edward C.: *Forty Years of Opera in Chicago,* 1930.

Morrison, Hugh: *Louis Sullivan, Prophet of Modern Architecture,* 1935.

Documents in the Roosevelt University Archives which include: the minutes of the Board of Directors and Executive Committee of the Chicago Auditorium Association, various transcripts of litigation between the Chicago Auditorium Association and the land owners (represented by trustees Mark S. Willing and Ambrose Cramer), and, in particular, "Testimony of Paul Mueller," *In the United States Circuit Court of Appeals for the Seventh Circuit, October Term, A. D. 1925, No., 3733 Chicago Auditorium Association vs. Mark Skinner Willing and the Northern Trust Company, as Trustees, etc., et al.* and testimony of John Goodridge, Mark S. Willing's representative and manager of the Auditorium Building Corporation.

A volume of photostated working drawings for the Auditorium Building (when construction began and when completed) and a scrapbook of clippings kept by the Auditorium Association in the Art Institute of Chicago Library.

22. Republican National Convention Hall
     Chicago Auditorium
     North side of Congress Street from Michigan to
     Wabash avenues
     Chicago, Illinois
     Adler & Sullivan
     1888
     Dismantled at close of convention
     Seating capacity: approximately 9,000 (7,603 fixed seats)

This hall was constructed within the as yet unfinished shell of the Auditorium Theatre. Seating was provided not only in the body of the theatre but on the stage as well. The room was illuminated by electric light bulbs hung from the exposed steel and cast iron framework of the building. The interior was decorated by an elaborate use of bunting.

At the conclusion of the convention, the various temporary arrangements of the hall were removed to permit the reinstallation of the scaffolding for the completion of the theatre's permanent finishes.

Sources:

The Chicago Tribune, June 9, 10, 12, and 20, 1888.

23. Grand Opera House
Northwest corner of Fourth and Main streets
Pueblo, Colorado
Adler & Sullivan
1888–90
No longer extant
Seating capacity: 993 (main floor: 485,
balcony: 269, gallery: 239, 8 boxes)

During May of 1888, at the behest of two Pueblo firms (Thatcher Brothers and Baxter & Creswell) who offered to provide the site and a significant amount of the capital for the construction of a large opera house, meetings were held with the citizens of Pueblo that culminated in the formation of The Pueblo Opera House Association on the 30th of that month. At a meeting of the directors of June 12, 1888, it was decided to employ Adler & Sullivan as architects for the building. They were awarded this commission because of the publicity they were then receiving as architects of the Chicago Auditorium. On June 30, either Adler or Sullivan (accounts differ) arrived in Pueblo with sketches of the proposed building and submitted them to the directors. By the end of the year, the drawings had been completed, and in January of 1889, the contracts for construction of the building were awarded. The work was directed by Henry W. French of the Adler & Sullivan office. During construction, both Adler and Sullivan came to Pueblo to examine the work. Excavation of the site began on February 5, 1889, and on October 9, 1890, the theatre was formally opened.

The principle facades were constructed of Manitou red stone on a gray granite base. It had a frontage of 120′ on Main Street and 190′ on Fourth Street and was 50′ high from the sidewalk to the underside of the eaves. The street frontage was four stories and contained stores on the first floor with offices and club rooms above. In line with the center of the triple-arched loggia which formed the entrance to the theatre on the Main Street side (but set some distance back) was an observation tower, 134′ from the sidewalk to the top of its tiled roof. Two similar one-story structures rose above the broad eaved tile roofs of the office and store block. One formed the top of the stage house, and the other housed a "summer garden."

The theatre was located at the rear of the site along two alleys that formed its western and northern limits. The auditorium was 78' wide and 80' deep. Its arrangement, although considerably smaller, was similar to that of the Chicago Auditorium (see entry 21). It had one level of boxes at each side of the proscenium, a main balcony of truncated horseshoe configuration, and a gallery above ran in a straight line. Although structural and ornamental columns were used within the body of the theatre, they were placed so as not to fall within areas of seating. This made it the first of Adler's theatres in which all possible obstructions to vision had been eliminated. The ceiling adjoining the proscenium was defined by a half-groin vault. This was to be the only example of such ceiling treatment in Adler's theatres, but he would use it again in his last executed auditorium, the Isaiah Temple in Chicago (see entry 31). Contemporary descriptions indicate the interior had an elaborate polychromatic decorative scheme. The stage was 78' wide, 33' 4" deep, 73' 9" from the floor to the rigging loft, and had a 32' proscenium.

At the north end of the building, immediately across the west alley and connected to it by a bridge, stood a separate brick building, 25' 4" by 37' 4", three stories and a basement high, that originally housed the boiler plant, dynamos, carpenter's workshop, scene storage, and fan chamber for the ventilation system. The theatre was illuminated by electricity and heated and ventilated by a system similar to that used in the Chicago Auditorium.

It seems no significant alterations, except the remodeling of the corner of the first floor, were made. The building was destroyed by fire on February 28, and March 1, 1922. A surviving part of the building was incorporated into the rear walls of the Colorado Building which now occupies the site.

Sources:

Englebrecht, Lloyd C.: "Adler & Sullivan's Pueblo Opera House: City Status for a New Town in the Rockies," *The Art Bulletin*, June 1985.
The Engineering Record, May 23, 30, 1891.
Pueblo Chieftain, April 30, 1890; October 10, 1890.
Pueblo Star-Journal, February 28, 1962.

24. K.A.M. (Kehilath Ansche Mayriv) Temple
(now Pilgrim Baptist Church)
Southeast corner of Indiana Avenue and 33rd Street
Chicago, Illinois
Adler & Sullivan
1890–91
Extant
Seating capacity: 1,500

Adler & Sullivan began work on this synagogue some time prior to the publication of a reference to the project in *The Inland Architect and News Record* of March 1890. Because Adler was a member of the K.A.M. congregation, and his father had been one of its most distinguished rabbis, the firm was given the commission to design it. It was dedicated on June 11, 1891.

The building has a frontage of 91′ on Indiana Avenue and 115′ on 33rd Street. In general, it is arranged much like the Zion Temple (catalog entry 19) with Sabbath school rooms on the first floor and the synagogue above, but whereas the shape of the auditorium in that building had been concealed behind twin towers, here the external form of the building was determined to a great extent by the configuration of the auditorium. The wood-clad barrel vault of the central part of the auditorium's ceiling forms a rectangular dome, pierced by windows, that is enclosed on the exterior by high walls (originally clad in ornamental sheet metal), which form a clerestory, which is capped by a high pyramidal roof. This feature, which rises above the building's three-story limestone walls, gives it a thoroughly centralized character unique in nineteenth-century synagogue architecture. Seating on the main floor of the auditorium is arranged in a semicircular fashion with a slight rise. A gallery, supported in part by cast iron columns, extends along the sides and rear of the room. The ark was originally set in a low semi-domed apse beneath the chamber of the organ pipes. Although the plan of the auditorium still retains a remnant of the half octagon end of Adler's earlier religious buildings, the visual effect of this feature is nullified by the prominence given to the barrel-vaulted ceiling and its supports.

For some reason, Adler determined that there should not be any columns in the gallery, even though they do occur on the main floor. To accomplish this, he designed the framing of the clerestory outer walls of the barrel vault as huge wood trusses bearing only on heavy piers at the corners. Over the years, however, these trusses began to sag, and intermediate column supports had to be added.

The building remained in use as a synagogue until 1920, when the congregation relocated, and the building was sold to its present owners, the Pilgrim Baptist Church. Although the exterior has been disfigured by the removal of all the ornamental sheet metal from the clerestory, much of the original interior finishes recently have been restored.

Sources:

Felsenthal, Bernhard and Herman Eliassof: *History of Kehilath Anshe Maarabh,* 1897.
Gutstein, Morris A.: *A Priceless Heritage,* 1953.
Meites, Hyman L.: *History of the Jews in Chicago,* 1924.
The Chicago Tribune, June 12, 1891.
The Inland Architect and News Record, March 1890; August 1891.
The Inter Ocean (Chicago), June 10, 1891.
The Reform Advocate, May 8, 1891; June 12, 1891.

25. *Deutsches Stadt Theater*
Northeast corner of Wells and Edison streets
Milwaukee, Wisconsin
Adler & Sullivan, Carl E. Hoffman
1890
No longer extant
Seating capacity: 1,200

Hermann Nunnemacher constructed a three-story masonry building with a frontage of 210′ on Wells Street, 76′ on Edison Street, and 80′ on Water Street and an overall height of 57′ from the sidewalk to the top of the cornice, in 1871. Almost its entire west end was taken up by the Grand Opera House, a theatre which had a seating capacity of 1,010 excluding the boxes.

At the beginning of 1890, Capt. Frederick Pabst acquired this building with the intention of remodeling the theatre as a new home for Milwaukee's principal German theatre company. By the end of April of 1890, Adler & Sullivan had prepared drawings for the complete reconstruction of that part of the building occupied by the theatre. Surviving portions of these drawings indicate that a fairly thorough but still somewhat preliminary scheme for the decorations had also been prepared. Unfortunately, Adler & Sullivan seem to have had no further involvement with the project. A local architect, Carl E. Hoffman, was employed to supervise construction of the theatre. The decorations were done in a Rococo manner under the direction of Otto Von Ernst (Capt. Pabst's son-in-law), in association with the painters Ferdinand Thomas and Franz Gehrte and the sculptor Carl Kuhns. Although Adler's arrangement of the interior remained basically intact in the hands of these men, the shape of the proscenium and its boxes was distorted in order to add a second level of boxes not called for in the Adler & Sullivan design. This revision was so poorly conceived that it was almost impossible to see the stage from the upper boxes, which led to their complete reconstruction in 1892. No changes were apparently made in the exterior of the original building in this remodeling. The remodeled theatre opened on September 17, 1890, under the name *Deutsches Stadt Theater,* the name of the former home of its new resident company.

The auditorium was 58' 4" wide and 89' 1" deep. The general arrangement of the seating was similar to that used in the Grand Opera House at Pueblo (catalog entry 23), with curved seating on the main floor and in the main balcony and a straight gallery above. The seating of the balcony no longer followed the curves of the traditional truncated horseshoe but was instead arranged in a semicircle. Apparently for reasons of economy, it was necessary to use columns within areas of seating on the main floor to support the balcony above. The stage was roughly 40' deep by 60' wide. The proscenium, as designed by Adler & Sullivan, would have been 29' wide and high.

On January 15, 1895, the theatre was totally destroyed by fire. Shortly thereafter, Pabst commissioned architect Otto Strack, who had remodeled the boxes in 1892, to design an entirely new and larger theatre for the site. This building, still named the Pabst Theater, opened on November 9, 1895. All that remained of the Nunnemacher Block was the four easternmost bays, which remained for many years but were then demolished.

Sources:

Andreas, A.T.: *History of Milwaukee, Wisconsin,* 1881.
The Inland Architect and News Record, May 1890.
The Milwaukee Journal, April 28, 1890; August 7, 1890; September 13, 1890; August 12, 1892; November 9, 1895.
Opening night souvenir program prepared by *Milwaukee Herald.*

26. Seattle Opera House
Northeast corner of Second and University streets
Seattle, Washington
Adler & Sullivan
1890
Never built
Seating capacity: 1,116 (parquet: 228,
parquet circle: 324, balcony: 364,
gallery: 300, 8 boxes)

Sources indicate that by the end of May of 1890, the Seattle Operahouse Company had acquired the above site and at the beginning of June, began excavation for the foundation of an opera house that would cost $200,000. In early August, Louis Sullivan visited Seattle and made some preliminary sketches for the building, the estimated cost of which had risen to $325,000 (this apparently included the cost of the land). Excavation work was still underway, and work on the foundation was then expected to begin early in September. Two telegrams sent in September by Adler & Sullivan to Judge Thomas Burke, the president of the company, indicate that the basic arrangement of the building had been determined and preparation of the working drawings was underway. By October 12th, Charles H. Bebb had arrived in Seattle with the drawings to take charge of the project as Adler & Sullivan's representative. The cost, apparently of the building alone, was then estimated to be $250,000. Although the excavation work had been underway since June, Bebb was not planning to begin work on the foundation for another week. Several building reports indicate that Adler & Sullivan were still working on the project in the last months of 1890, and a perspective and three plans of their design appear in the January 1891 issue of *The Inland Architect and News Record,* but nothing was heard after that. It was apparently one of many victims of the depression which afflicted Seattle from 1891 to 1897.

Fortunately, a longitudinal section and another set of plans, in addition to those mentioned above (now in the Northwest Architectural Archives of the University of Minnesota Libraries), have survived. It is possible to get a good understanding of the principal features of the proposed building as designed by Adler & Sullivan. The stage was to have been roughly 70′ wide and 35′ deep. The proscenium was to have been 32′ wide, and the height of the stage from the floor to the rigging loft was to have been 71′. The auditorium was to have been approximately 70′ wide and 87′ deep. Its general arrangement was practically the same as that of the Stadt Theater at Milwaukee (catalog entry 25), with the same semicircular balcony and straight gallery. The curve of the balcony parapet was, however, to have extended forward to define the walls as well as the ceiling adjoining the proscenium. This would have given the auditorium an almost spherical character. The building was to have had a frontage of 180′ on Second Street and 108′ on University Street. The auditorium was to have been concealed behind a five-story and attic apartment hotel. The location of the stage was to have been marked on the Second Street front by a seven-story wing which was to contain stores on the first floor with dressing rooms and other auxiliary stage facilities above. The main entrance to the theatre and apartments above was to have been off a triple arched loggia at the base of a twelve-story tower that would have risen to a height of 204′ above the first floor level. Because of the extreme incline of the site, the parquet and stage were to have been located at the second floor level, with the first floor occupied primarily by stores and a restaurant.

Sources:

The Economist, November 28, 1890.
The Inland Architect and News Record, December 1890; January 1891.
The Realestate and Building Journal, October 18, 1890.
The Seattle Post Intelligencer, May 25, 1890; June 19, 1890.
The Seattle Telegraph, August 16, 1890; September 14, 1890; October 12, 1890.

Information supplied to the author by Jeffrey K. Ochsner and Dennis Anderson of Seattle, who were at this writing preparing an article on this building.

27. *Schiller Theater* Building
   (German Opera House Building)
   64 West Randolph Street
   Chicago, Illinois
   Adler & Sullivan
   1891–92
   No longer extant
   Seating capacity: 1,270 (main floor: 600,
   balcony and gallery: 670, 6 boxes)

The idea of constructing this theatre appears to date from the latter part of 1889. The first public announcements of the project seem to have been two articles which appeared in the *Illinois Staat Zeitung* on March 28, and 29, 1890. These indicate that the promoters had formed the German Opera House Company on March 28, 1890 and acquired an option to lease the property at the above location on which they proposed to erect a twelve-story, steel frame, fireproof buliding. The site under consideration at that time (and also that on which the building was ultimately erected) had a frontage of 80′ 4″ on Randolph Street and a depth of 181′ 6″, with an alley at the rear.

By October of 1890, the promoters had leased the land on Randolph Street and been offered a lease on the property adjoining it to the east on the alley and facing Dearborn Street. On this site, as thus expanded, it was proposed to erect a twelve-story L-shaped office and theatre building. It was not until January of 1891 that the German Opera House Company actually received its charter and selected its board of directors. An entry in *The Economist* of January 24, 1891, indicates that no decision had yet been made regarding the acquisition of the Dearborn Street property, and Adler & Sullivan had just been selected as architects on the basis of an informal vote which was confirmed several days later. There is no known evidence to suggest that they were involved with the project before January of 1891.

Entries in *The Economist* of February 7, and 14, 1891 indicate that by early February the idea of using the Dearborn Street property had been abandoned. These entries also describe what appears to have been Adler & Sullivan's first design for the building. The front elevation was to have taken up the full width of the lot for the first eight floors, above which its width was to be reduced to form a fourteen-story tower capped by a "dome shaped spire with lookout windows in front." The theatre was to have been substantially the same as in the executed building. Club, dining, rehearsal, kitchen, and banquet rooms were to be located in the top three floors of the twelve-story portion of the building between the tower and the alley. The plans were being drawn in such a way as to permit the use of the upper floors for either hotel rooms or offices. A perspective of this design was published in *King's Handbook of the United States* by the Matthews-Northrup Co. of Buffalo, New York, in 1891.

On May 3, and 4, 1891, most of the Chicago newspapers carried descriptions of the new building, ground breaking for which had taken place on May 1, 1891. Many of these descriptions are accompanied by the same illustration that shows the height of every section of the building had been increased by one story, an arcaded balcony had been added across the front of the entire second floor, and a massive cornice and domed cupola had replaced the similar but more subdued features at the top of the tower in the earlier design. The interior remained as described earlier except the club rooms, kitchen, etc. had all been moved up one floor to remain in the top stories. The remainder of the building, at this stage, was to be taken up by a hotel. Aside from a further increase of two stories in the height of the tower and the abandonment of the hotel in favor of offices (which had been determined by the time construction got under way in the summer of 1891), no further significant changes were made in the design.

The extremely narrow site (sandwiched in between other buildings) on which the building was to be built created as many problems for Adler as he found in the design of the Chicago Auditorium. In order to obtain sufficient light in the offices above the theatre, most of which had to face the adjoining buildings, it was necessary to set their exterior walls somewhat back from the lot lines. In this process, he created the first "setbacks" ever used in tall office building construction. As the theatre had to occupy the first six floors (except the very front) and the very rear of the seventh floor for its

81

rigging loft, it was necessary to carry the entire weight of the offices above upon a system of massive steel trusses at the seventh and eighth floors that rested on the outer masonry bearing walls of the theatre and stage. Although this was the first of Adler & Sullivan's buildings to be otherwise entirely of light-weight steel frame construction, the load concentrated on these walls was still enormous. To support it adequately, Adler devised, in consultation with architect Solon S. Beman (who had just recently used pile foundations under the tower of his Grand Central Depot) the first such foundations ever used under a tall office building. Not only was Adler's solution to the problems of this building a great functional and structural triumph, but its unique design was also one of the finest produced by the firm of Adler & Sullivan.

Originally the building was to have been known as the German Opera House Building. By the opening of the theatre on the evening of September 29, 1892, the name had been changed to the *Schiller Theater* Building.

The auditorium was roughly 62′ wide and 88′ deep. It was heated and ventilated by a system similar to that used in the Chicago Auditorium (catalog entry 21) and entirely illuminated by electricity. Its arrangement was identical to that already developed in the designs for the Stadt Theater (catalog entry 25) and the Seattle Opera House (catalog entry 26) with a semicircular main balcony and straight gallery above, but, whereas the ceiling adjoining the proscenium in both of these earlier designs consisted of a basically smooth trumpet-like surface divided into shallow panels by projecting ribs, here a series of radiating full arches (with ventilating grilles serving as their spandrels) was used. The steel frame of the building provided sufficient anchorage for cantilever framing to be used to support the main balcony. This made it possible for Adler to again eliminate all possible obstructions as he had in the Opera House at Pueblo (catalog entry 23). In this room and its ancillary spaces, Sullivan applied what was probably his most elaborate scheme of polychrome stenciling and plaster ornament.

The stage was roughly 34′ deep and 78′ wide. The proscenium was 29′ 8″ high and wide, and the height of the stage from the floor to the rigging loft was 70′ 11″.

Several years after its dedication, the theatre was renamed the Dearborn Theatre, which in turn was changed to the Garrick Theatre. In the 1920s, it was converted into a movie house. After a lengthy fight for its preservation, it was demolished in 1961. Much of its ornament was salvaged and then distributed to museums. A multi-story parking garage today stands on the pile foundations of the Schiller and incorporates a piece of the Schiller's buff-brown terra-cotta into its hideous facade.

Sources:

Adler, Dankmar: "Piling for Isolated Foundations Adjoining to Walls—A Discussion," *The Inland Architect and News Record,* January 1893.
Anonymous: *Industrial Chicago,* The Building Interests, vol. 1, 1891.
Condit, Carl W.: *The Chicago School of Architecture,* 1964.
————. "The Structural System of Adler and Sullivan's Garrick Theater Building," *Technology and Culture,* Fall, 1964.
Flinn, John J.: *The Standard Guide of Chicago,* 1893.
King, Moses: *King's Handbook of the United States,* 1891.
Sprague, Paul E.: "Adler and Sullivan's Schiller Building," *The Prairie School Review,* Second Quarter, 1965.
Abendpost (Chicago), April 10, 1890; May 4, 1890.
The American Architect and Building News, February 4, 1893.
The Architectural Record, January –March 1892.
Architecture and Building, October 24, 1891.
The Chicago Evening Post, September 29, 1891.
The Chicago Times, September 30, 1891.
The Chicago Tribune, October 30, 1890; May 3, 1891.
The Economist, April 12, 1890; January 1, 10, 24, 30, 1891; February 7, 14, 1891; March 21, 1891; May 9, 30, 1891; July 3, 1891; September 5, 1891; May 23, 1893.
Illinois Staat-Zeitung (Chicago), March 28, 29, 1890; April 8, 1890; May 12, 14, 19, 1890; October 27, 1890; May 4, 1891.
The Inland Architect and News Record, June 1891; February 1892.
The Inter Ocean (Chicago), May 3, 1891; September 30, 1892.

28. Republican National Convention Hall
    Minneapolis Industrial Exposition Building
    North corner of Central Avenue and Main Street
    Minneapolis, Minnesota
    Adler & Sullivan, consultants; Warren Hayes
    1892
    No longer extant
    Seating capacity: 11,500 (main floor: 8,500,
    gallery: 3,000)

Soon after Minneapolis had secured the convention, Warren Hayes, a local architect employed by the convention committee, completed plans for the remodeling of the interior of the Exposition Building in Minneapolis into the convention hall. This large structure, designed by architect Isaac Hudson, Sr. and erected in 1886, was over 400′ × 500′. The chairman of the national convention committee found the Hayes design to be defective, and Adler was called in as a consultant to the national committee to prepare an alternative design. The design which he prepared was, however, regarded as too expensive by the local committee, primarily because it required the removal of a substantial portion of the third floor of the building. In order to overcome their differences, representatives of both committees met in Minneapolis on February 8, 1892, and worked out a compromise that apparently satisfied Adler. Because of his proximity to the project, Hayes was put in charge of executing it.

The area reserved for the auditorium at the center of the building was 235′ × 238′. The delegates were in the column-free space, below a huge glazed skylight, at the center of this area. A raked gallery (resting on the second floor of the building) and raked seating (on the main floor below) was provided around all four sides of the room for the audience. Although this was apparently the largest convention hall constructed in America up to that time, its numerous columns made it difficult for many in the hall to properly observe the convention.

The convention hall seems to have remained intact until the following year, when another smaller auditorium was constructed in the center of the building. The Exposition Building was turned into a mail-order warehouse in 1903, long after decreasing revenues had forced the annual exposition to be discontinued. In 1940, after it had stood vacant for several years, the building was purchased by the Coca-Cola Bottling Co., which demolished all but its main tower. The latter was demolished in 1946, when construction of a new bottling plant, postponed by World War II, was resumed on the site.

Sources:

Anonymous: "The Exposition Building 1886 to 1939," *Hennepin County History*, October 1953.
Holmquist, June Drenning: "Convention City, The Republicans in Minneapolis 1892," *Minnesota History*, June 1951.
The Minneapolis Times, May 29, 1892.
The Minneapolis Times–Tribune, February 12, 1940.
The Minneapolis Tribune, February 9, 1892; March 12, 1946; May 14, 1946.

29. Trocadero Music Hall
    First Regiment Armory
    Northwest corner of Sixteenth Street
    and Michigan Avenue
    Chicago, Illinois
    Adler & Sullivan
    1893
    No longer extant

The Economist of March 4, 1893 reported Adler & Sullivan were then working on the Trocadero Music Hall. Their client was the Trocadero Amusement and Restaurant Company, headed by the renowned Dr. Florence Ziegfeld (Florenz Ziegfeld, Sr., founder and President of the Chicago Musical College and father of the showman).

On the morning of April 25, 1893, five days before it was to open, a fire apparently started in some electrical equipment on the stage. It completely destroyed the nearly finished auditorium and all but a small portion of the armory. The armory was a massive fortress-like building designed by architects Burnham and Root in 1889 and completed in 1891. In order to provide for an entirely column-free drill hall at the ground floor, large three-hinged arches originating at grade were provided to carry the roof and all the upper floors and galleries. It was the failure of these arches when exposed to the intense heat that caused the entire structure to collapse in upon itself.

From the few fragmentary remarks in the press just before and after its destruction, one can see this auditorium was a relatively inexpensive remodeling of the drill hall. A stage with a proscenium arch made of staff, the material which had just been used to face the recently completed buildings of the Columbian Exposition, had been constructed, and the enclosing walls of the auditorium were of pine. It is not clear whether any alterations were made to the existing construction of the armory.

Immediately after the fire, a contract for the use of Battery "D" Armory, just north of the newly completed Art Institute Building, was secured, and the enterprise opened there according to the original schedule. There is no evidence to connect Adler & Sullivan with the Battery "D" Trocadero, and since it was fitted up in such haste, their involvement, if any, would have been minimal.

Sources:

Hoffman, Donald: *The Architecture of John Wellborn Root,* 1973.
The Economist, March 4, 1893.
The Chicago Daily News, April 25, 1893.
The Chicago Tribune, April 23, 25, 26, 1893.

30. Republican National Convention Hall
    North side of Clark Avenue between
    Twelfth and Thirteenth streets
    St. Louis, Missouri
    Dankmar Adler, consultant; Isaac E. Taylor
    1896
    No longer extant
    Seating capacity: 14,000
    (main floor: 8,000, gallery: 6,000)

This convention hall was constructed from drawings prepared by St. Louis architect Isaac Taylor for the convention committee of the Business-Men's League of St. Louis. Its similarity to the convention hall at Minneapolis (catalog entry 28) indicates that Taylor had been greatly influenced by that design. That may explain why Adler found Taylor's drawings for the most part correct and made only minor changes when he visited St. Louis at the beginning of March of 1896 as consultant to the Hall Committee of the National Republican Committee.

The main block of this wood frame building was 260′ long and 180′ wide. A raked gallery, with raked seating below for the audience, extended around all four sides of the interior. The wood columns which supported the parapet of the galleries also supported the clear span roof over the delegates' area at the center of the building, the floor of which was level.

As originally approved, Taylor's drawings called for enclosures around the stairways located beyond the main walls of the auditoriums and a rather restrained ornamental treatment of the facades. By mid-April of 1896, these features had, however, been eliminated. Following the convention, the building was demolished.

Sources:

The Economist, March 28, 1896; August 1, 1896.
The Chicago Tribune, March 8, 1896.
The Republic (St. Louis), March 6, 1896; April 19, 1896.

31.   Isaiah Temple (now Ebenezer Baptist Church)
      Southeast corner of Vincennes Avenue
      and Forty-fifth Street
      Chicago, Illinois
      Dankmar Adler
      1898–99
      Extant
      Seating capacity: 1,200

Early in 1898, the Isaiah Congregation, which was founded in 1895, purchased the property as a site for a synagogue. An entry in *The Reform Advocate* of April 16, 1898 indicates that by that date they had retained Adler as architect for the building. The cornerstone was laid on September 11, 1898, and the synagogue was dedicated in three days of celebrations beginning on March 17, 1899.

This Palladian styled building has a frontage of 97′ on Vincennes Avenue and 127′ on Forty-fifth Street. The auditorium occupies the entire front of the building (facing Vincennes Avenue), and the two-story and basement rear portion was originally used by a Sabbath school. The auditorium is roughly 80′ long and 90′ wide. The seating on the main floor is arranged in a curvilinear fashion, and a balcony extends along the side and rear walls. The ceiling consists of a coffered elliptical barrel vault which runs width-wise across the room and is intersected at the ark and rear ends by lesser full barrel vaults. The whole effect is similar to that which had been created by the proscenium of the Grand Opera House at Pueblo (catalog entry 23).

The building remained in use as a synagogue until 1921. The congregation then relocated, and the building was sold to its present owners, the Ebenezer Baptist Church. The interior remains much as it was when originally conceived, but the exterior has been defaced by the addition of a large metal fence, covering the entrance, and the removal of the original stained glass window above.

Sources:

Anonymous: *Our First Century 1852–1952, Temple Isaiah Israel,* 1952.

The Chicago Journal, March 18, 1899.

The Inter Ocean (Chicago), June 25, 1899.

The Reform Advocate, April 16, 1898; March 18, 1899; September 10, 17, 1899.

32. Autumn Festival Stadium

33. Exposition Building
     Site bounded by Ontario and St. Clair streets,
     Grand Avenue and Lake Shore Drive
     Chicago, Illinois
     Dankmar Adler
     1899
     Never built
     Seating capacity: Stadium: 50,000; Exposition Building:
     13,500 permanent seats (main floor: 9,000, gallery:
     4,500), room for 46,500 temporary seats

In June of 1899, the North Side Business Men's Association proposed that the property at the above location, known as the Ogden Tract, be used as the site for a stadium which was to be the principal attraction of a proposed city-wide Autumn Festival, then in the planning stages. Although sites in other parts of the city were being considered, the North Siders appear to have been the most well-organized. The only flaw in their proposed site was the lack of a suitable trolley line. They proposed to have the City Council approve a franchise for a new line to connect the site with existing lines. By July 14, 1899, however, factionalism had become so great that a quorum could not be assembled in the City Council to consider the matter. The Festival Association then dropped the stadium idea from its plans. On the day the trolley issue was to be considered, several of the newspapers carried a notice that Adler had prepared a design for a stadium to be used for musical events, seating 50,000 people, that could be erected in six weeks. Although it is not known for whom or under what circumstances Adler prepared this design, he was not the only architect interested in the project. Both architects Arthur Hercz and Louis Guenzel had prepared earlier, unsolicited designs that had been published in the newspapers. Unfortunately, no record of Adler's stadium design survives.

The North Side Business Men's Association, aware they might not get the stadium, had announced as early as June 8, 1899, it intended to erect a permanent exposition building on the Ogden Tract if the stadium did not materialize. On August

6, 1899, Charles F. Gillman, president of the association, unveiled plans prepared by Adler for this new project. The proposed structure was to have been 350' wide and 1,200' long. Along one of the long sides of a great central, clear span hall was to have been a structure to house permanent main floor and gallery seating. The entire structure was to have had a steel frame and been covered with a skin of stone, brick, and terra-cotta. Since discrepancies exist between the published views of the building (the number of bays and the fenestration of the end pavilions in the elevation are different in the plan), it seems Adler had prepared more than one completed design. This project was also abandoned shortly after it was unveiled.

Sources:

Anonymous: *Chicago Autumn Festival, October 4 to 11, 1899*, 1899.

The American Architect and Building News, July 8, 1899; August 19, 1899.

The Chicago Times-Herald, August 6, 1899.

The Chicago Tribune, June 25, 1899; July 14, 15, 1899; August 6, 1899.

The Inter Ocean (Chicago), June 18, 1899; July 8, 14, 15, 1899; August 6, 1899.

1. St. James Episcopal Church, Chicago

The reconstruction of this still extant building after the Chicago Fire was definitely the work of Burling & Adler. It has only a remote similarity to other churches known to have been designed by Adler, and is not among those buildings of the firm with which he claimed to be involved. John Edelmann appears to have been responsible for most of the project.

2. Grace Methodist Church, Chicago

Although this no longer extant church was the work of Burling & Adler, a description of it in *The Inter Ocean* of May 5, 1873, credits its design to Burling who was one of the congregation's members.

3. Tabor Grand Opera House, Denver, Colorado

A description of Adler's Academy of Music at Kalamazoo, Michigan erroneously credits the design of the no longer extant Tabor Grand Opera House at Denver to him. While this building, which was constructed in 1880, has a definite resemblance to the work of Adler's firm at that time, it was actually designed by Edbrooke and Burnham of Chicago.

4. People's Theatre, Chicago

A notice in *The Inland Architect and News Record* of June, 1884, indicates Adler & Sullivan were preparing drawings for this theatre for Jonathan Clark, a prominent contractor. Although Clark did actually erect it, a photograph of the exterior and other evidence indicates that Adler & Sullivan's role in the project was extremely limited (if, in fact, they were actually involved). Once located on the east side of State Street between Congress and Harrison streets, it was demolished in the 1930s.

5. Music Hall (Carnegie Hall) New York, New York

A number of contemporary sources, including the program for the first performances given in this famous building state that Adler & Sullivan were employed as consultant architects to William Burnet Tuthill, the architect in charge of the project. Although Adler was apparently retained to advise on acoustics and ventilation, the extent of his involvement with this project is unclear. The auditorium, where one would expect to see his contribution, bears little similarity to Adler's other auditoriums and was constructed with little regard for the *isacoustic curve* principle that Adler considered essential to good acoustical design.

1. Main Building, The College of Wooster, Wooster, Ohio.

2. Main Building. Interior of Kauke Chapel.

3. First Methodist Church, Kalamazoo, Michigan.

4. Wilcoxon Opera House, Freeport, Illinois.

5. Second Presbyterian Church, La Porte, Indiana.

6. Methodist Church Block, Chicago.

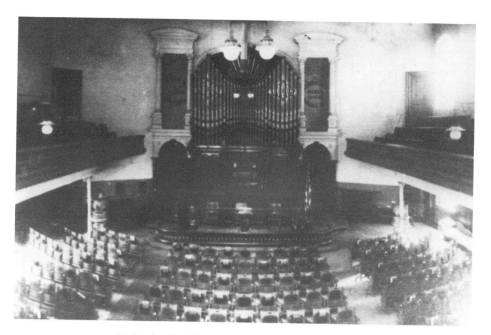

7. Methodist Church Block. Interior toward front.

8. Methodist Church Block. Interior toward rear.

9. Unity Church, Chicago. Exterior as proposed by Burling & Adler

10. Kingsbury Music Hall, Chicago. Interior.

11. First Congregational Church, Oak Park, Illinois.

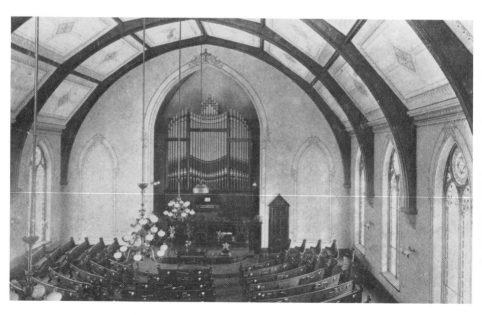

12. First Congregational Church. Interior.

13. Sinai Temple, Chicago. Exterior after remodeling of 1892.

14. Sinai Temple. Interior after remodeling of 1892.

15. Central Music Hall, Chicago.

16. Central Music Hall. Interior toward rear.

17. Central Music Hall. Stage and organ.

18. Central Music Hall. Apollo Hall after remodeling of 1890.

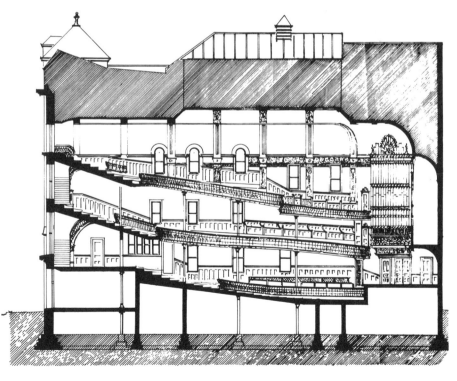

19. Central Music Hall. Longitudinal section.

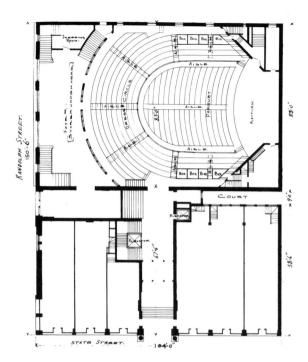

20. Central Music Hall. Plan of main floor.

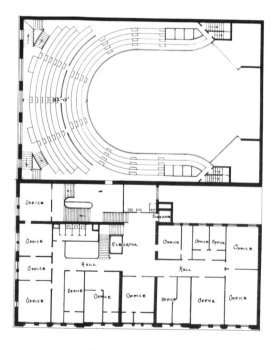

21. Central Music Hall. Plan of third floor showing balcony.

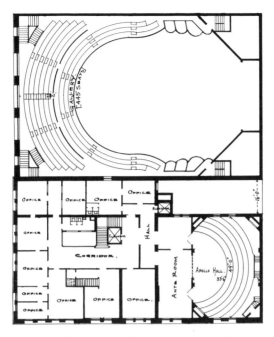

22. Central Music Hall. Plan of sixth floor showing gallery and Apollo Hall.

23. Grand Opera House, Chicago. Proscenium boxes.

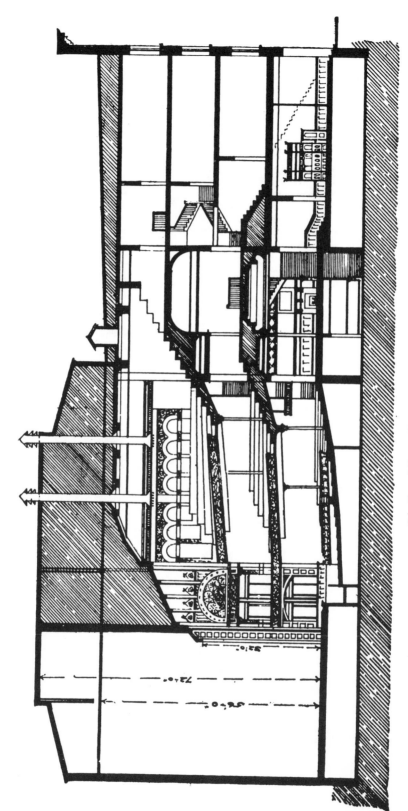

24. Grand Opera House. Longitudinal section.

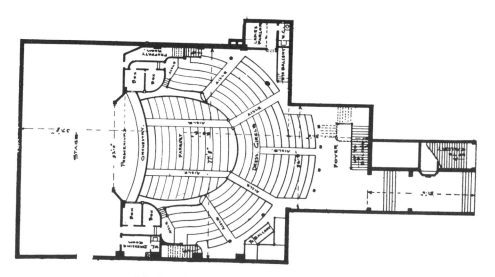

25. Grand Opera House. Plan of main floor.

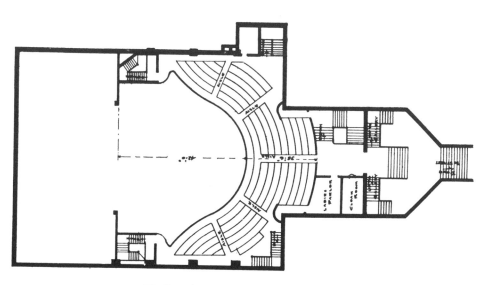

26. Grand Opera House. Plan of gallery.

111

27. Academy of Music, Kalamazoo, Michigan.

28. Academy of Music. Proscenium and boxes.

113

29. Academy of Music. Interior toward rear.

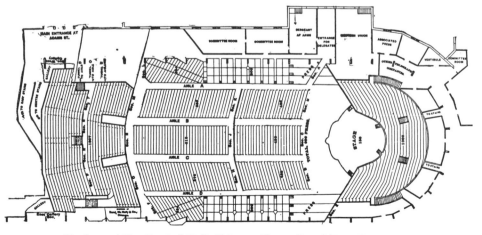

30. Second May Festival Hall, Chicago. Plan at Republican Convention.

31. Hooley's Theatre, Chicago. Interior.

32. McVicker's Theatre, Chicago. Exterior of upper four floors showing re-modeling and addition of 1885.

33. McVicker's Theatre. Vestibule in 1885.

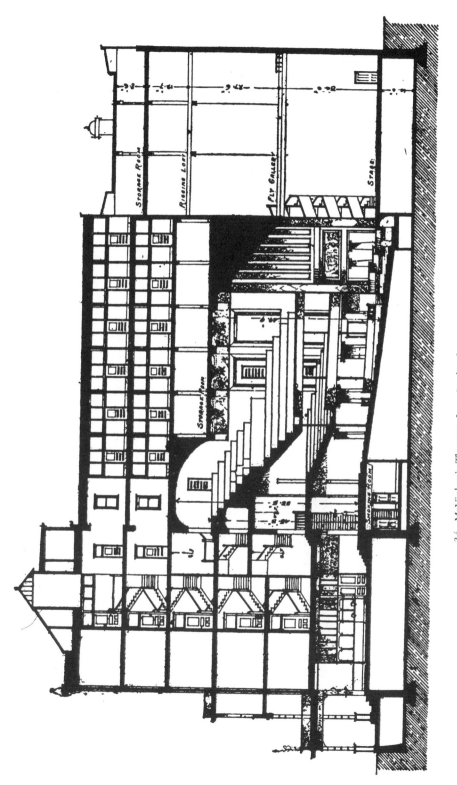

34. McVicker's Theatre. Longitudinal section in 1891.

35. McVicker's Theatre. Proscenium boxes in 1891.

118

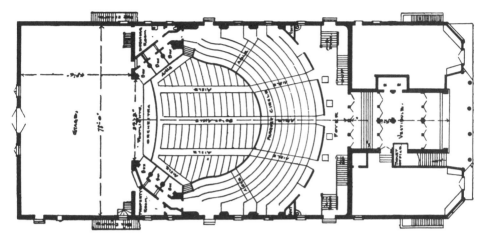

36. McVicker's Theatre. Plan of first floor.

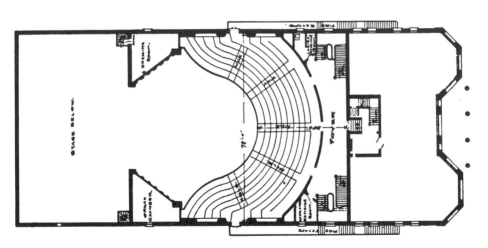

37. McVicker's Theatre. Plan of balcony.

38. Opera Festival Hall, Chicago. Detail of boxes.

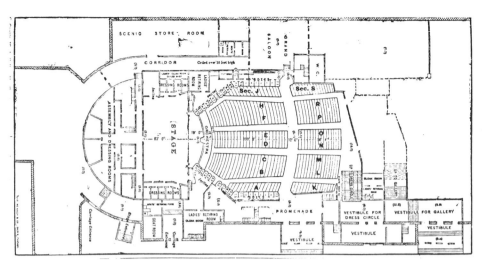

39. Opera Festival Hall. Plan of main floor.

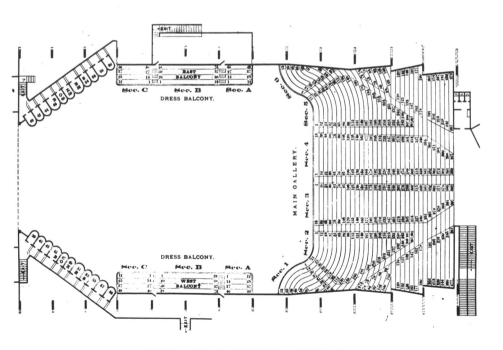

40. Opera Festival Hall. Plan of balconies.

41. Zion Temple, Chicago. Original design.

42. Zion Temple.

43. Zion Temple. Interior.

44. North American Saengerfest Hall, Milwaukee.

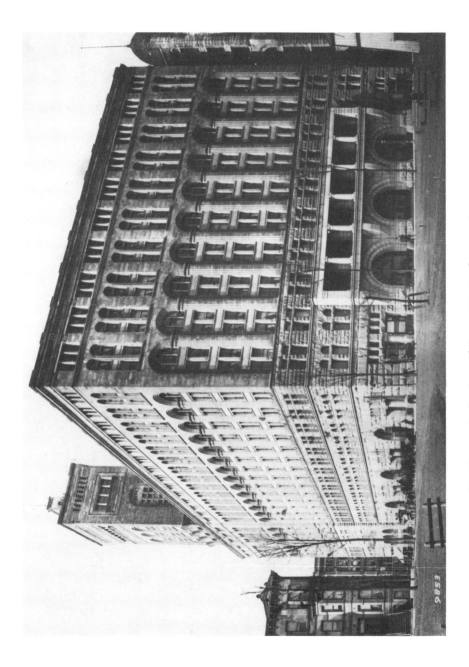

45. Chicago Auditorium, Chicago. Exterior from southeast.

46. Chicago Auditorium. Theatre lobby.

47. Chicago Auditorium. Upper foyer of theatre.

128

48. Chicago Auditorium. Interior of theatre toward proscenium.

49. Chicago Auditorium. Organ and boxes of theatre.

50. Chicago Auditorium. Interior of theatre from stage.

51. Chicago Auditorium. Interior of theatre with galleries closed off.

52. Chicago Auditorium. Interior of theatre at reopening in 1967.

53. Chicago Auditorium. Main floor of stage.

54. Chicago Auditorium. Lower level of stage.

55. Chicago Auditorium. Hotel lobby.

56. Chicago Auditorium. Staircase in hotel lobby.

57. Chicago Auditorium. Hotel reception room.

58. Chicago Auditorium. Hotel dining room.

59. Chicago Auditorium. North end of hotel dining room.

140

60. Chicago Auditorium. Hotel banquet hall.

61. Chicago Auditorium. Recital hall above theatre.

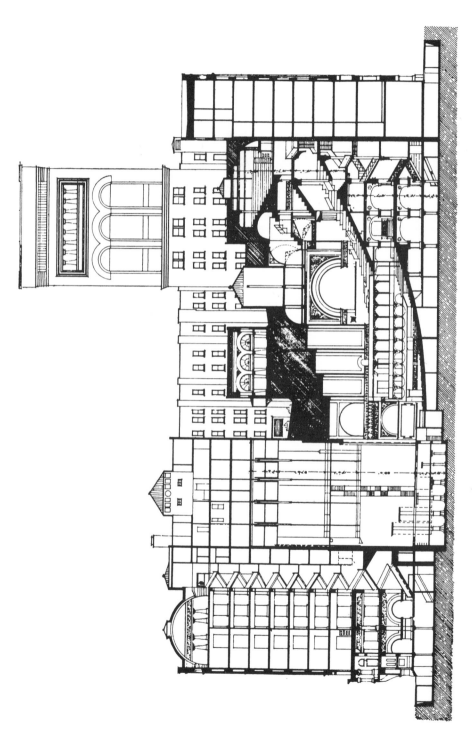

62. Chicago Auditorium. Longitudinal section.

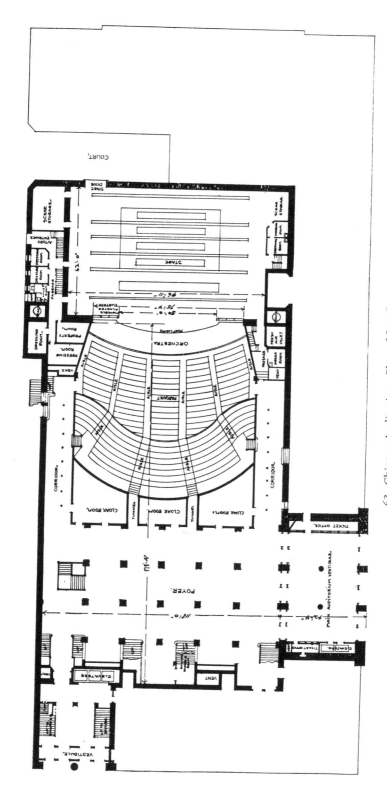

63. Chicago Auditorium. Plan of first floor.

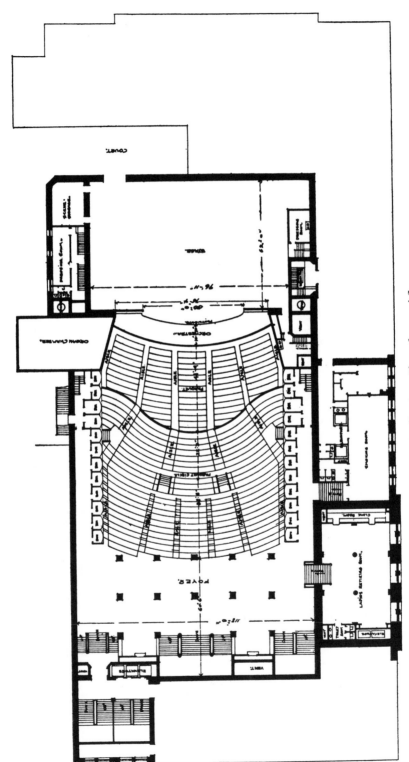

64. Chicago Auditorium. Plan of second floor.

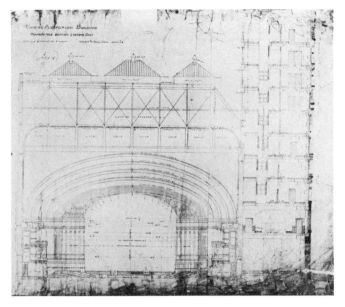

65. Chicago Auditorium. Transverse section when construction began.

66. Republican National Convention Hall, Chicago.

67. Grand Opera House, Pueblo, Colorado.

68. Grand Opera House. Proscenium.

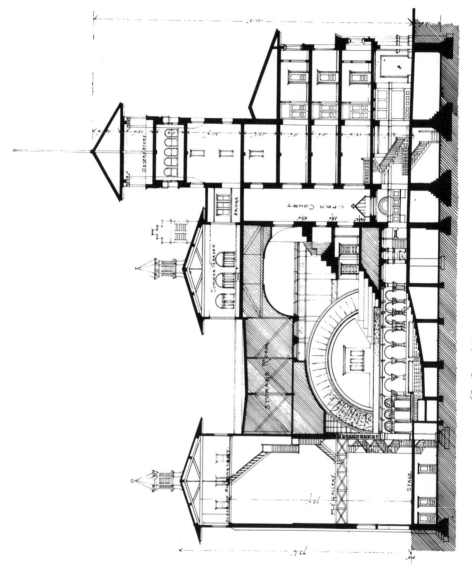

69. Grand Opera House. Longitudinal section.

70. Grand Opera House. Plan of main floor.

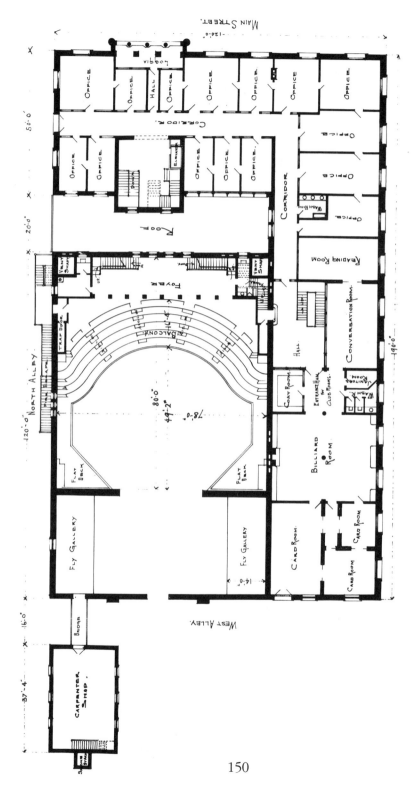

71. Grand Opera House. Plan of balcony.

150

72. K. A. M. Temple, Chicago.

73. K. A. M. Temple. Interior.

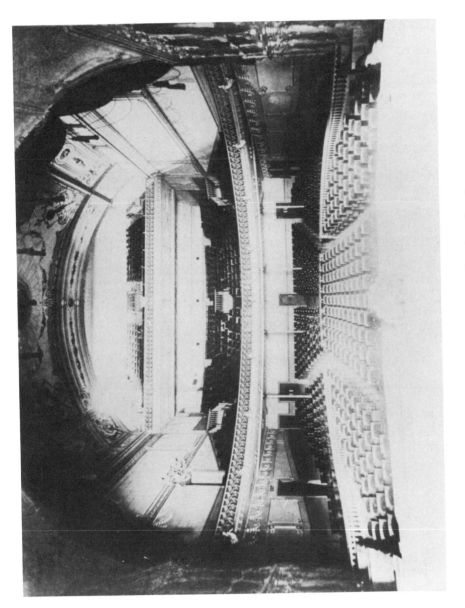

74. Deutsches Stadt Theater, Milwaukee. Interior.

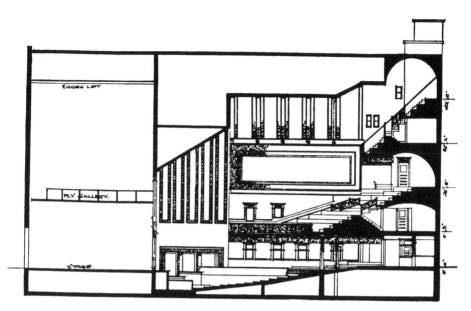

75. Deutsches Stadt Theater. Longitudinal section.

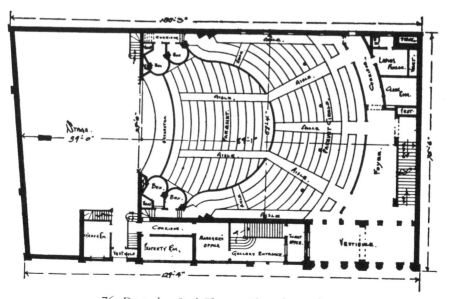

76. Deutsches Stadt Theater. Plan of main floor.

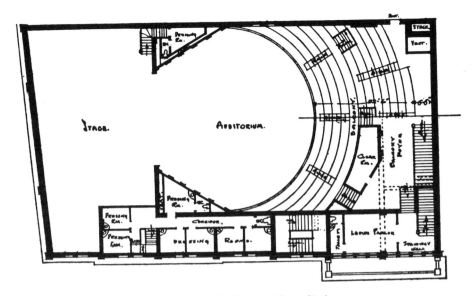

77. Deutsches Stadt Theater. Plan of balcony.

78. Deutsches Stadt Theater. Elevation of proscenium.

79. Seattle Opera House, Seattle, Washington.

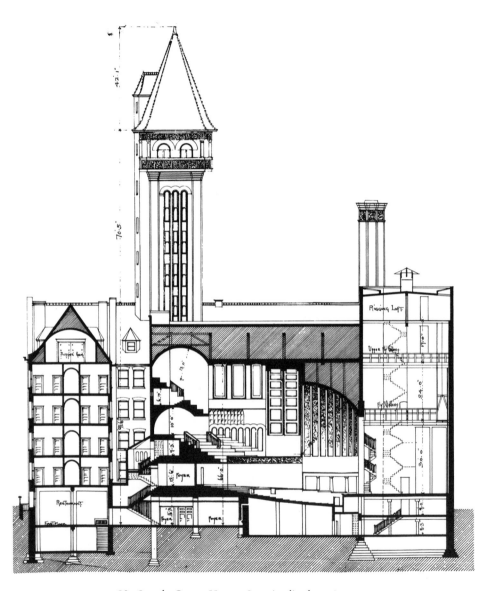

80. Seattle Opera House. Longitudinal section.

156

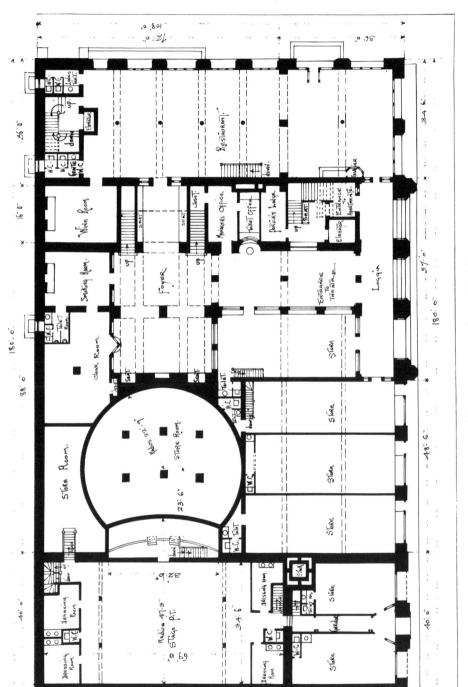

81. Seattle Opera House. Plan of first floor.

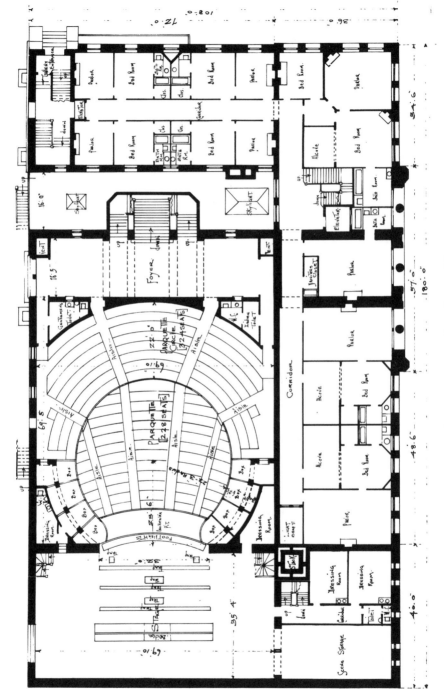

82. Seattle Opera House. Plan of second floor.

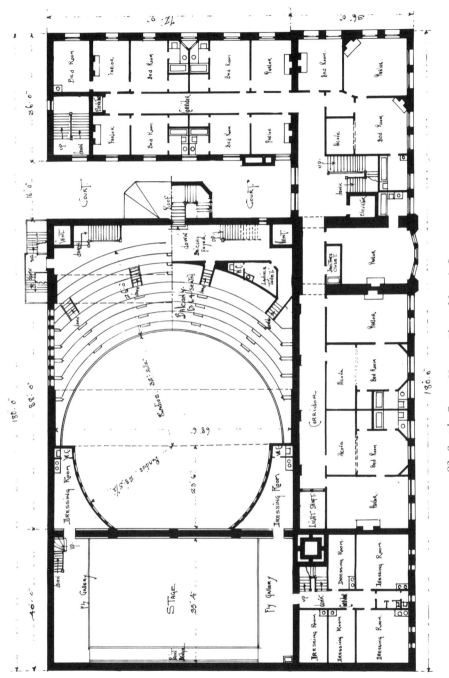

83. Seattle Opera House. Plan of fourth floor.

159

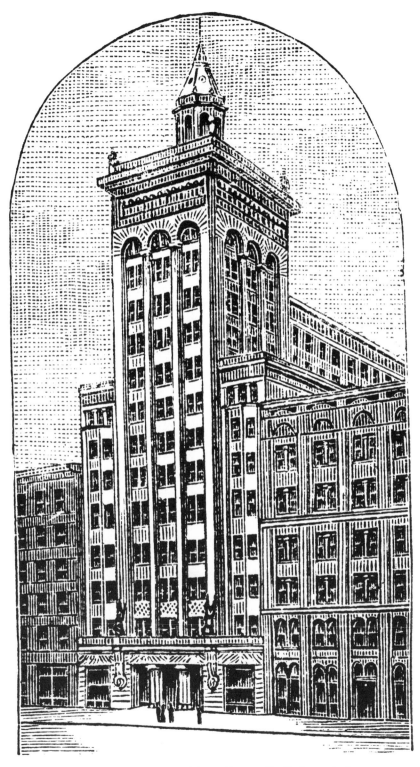

84. Schiller Theater Building, Chicago. Preliminary design.

85. Schiller Theater Building. Final design.

86. Schiller Theater Building. Theatre boxes in 1890s.

87. Schiller Theater Building. Stage.

88. Schiller Theater Building. Theatre interior in 1950s.

164

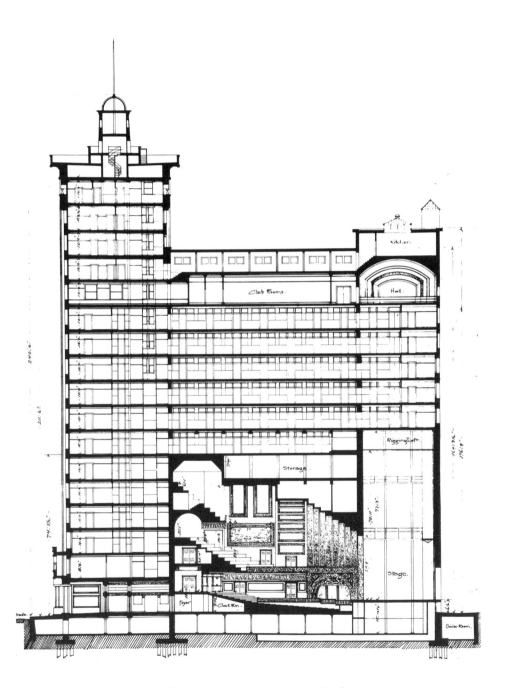

89. Schiller Theater Building. Longitudinal section.

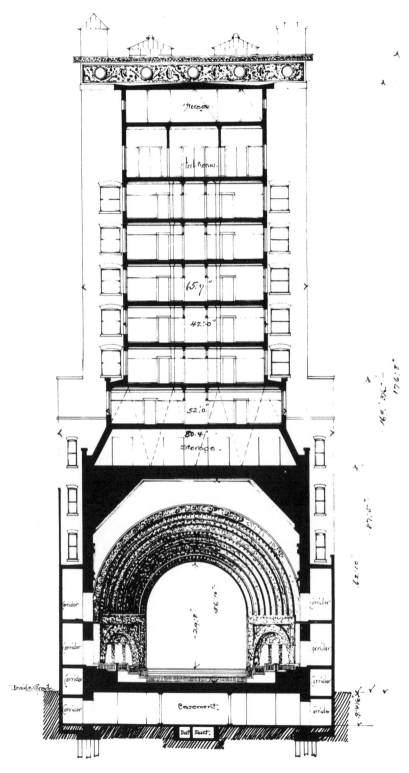

90. Schiller Theater Building. Transverse section.

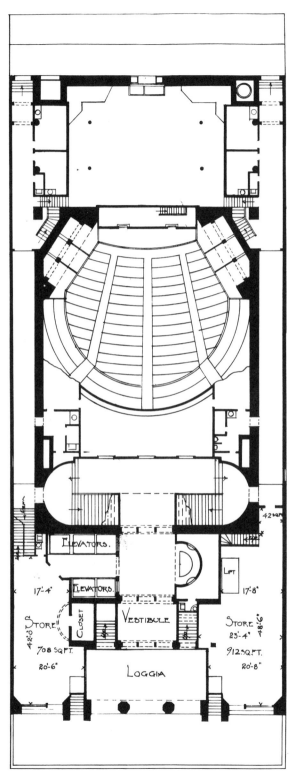

91. Schiller Theater Building. Plan of first floor.

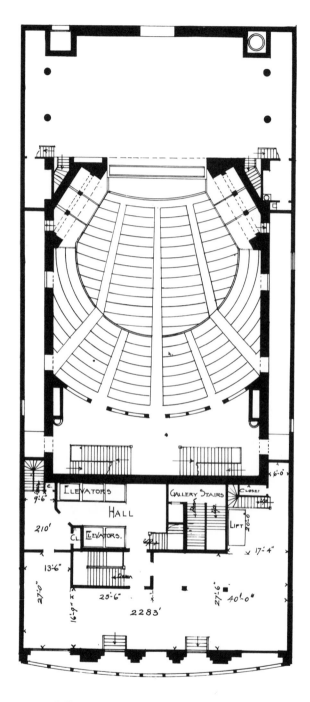

92. Schiller Theater Building. Plan of second floor.

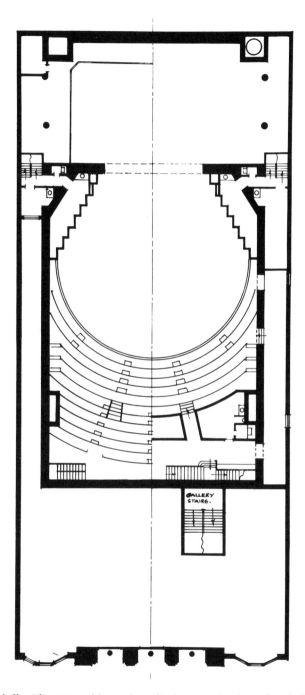

93. Schiller Theater Building. Plan of balcony at third and fourth floors.

GALLERY
STAIRS.

94. Republican National Convention Hall, Minneapolis.

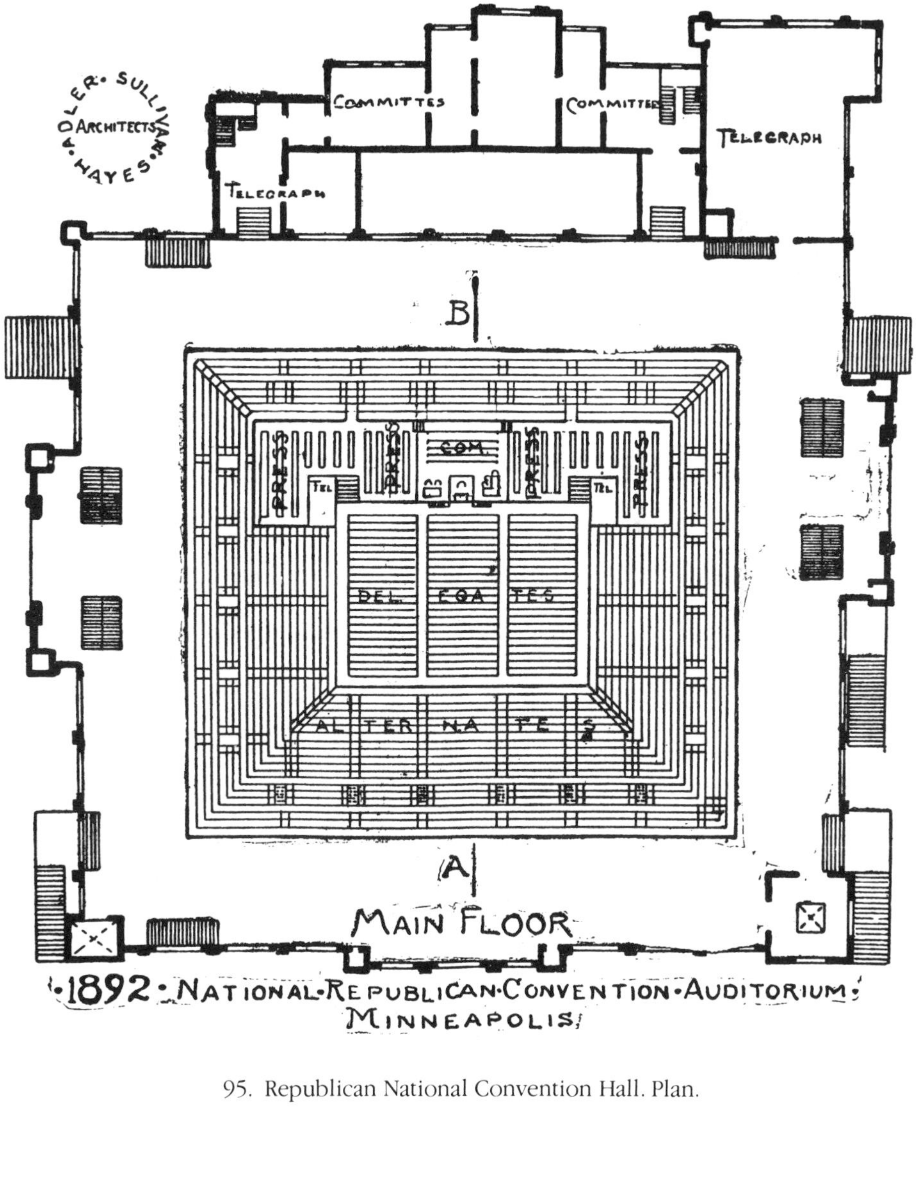
ADLER · SULLIVAN
ARCHITECTS
HAYES
COMMITTES
COMMITTEE
TELEGRAPH
TELEGRAPH
B
PRESS
PRESS
COM
PRESS
PRESS
TEL
TEL
DEL EGA TES
AL TER NA TES
A
MAIN FLOOR
·1892· NATIONAL·REPUBLICAN·CONVENTION·AUDITORIUM·
MINNEAPOLIS

95. Republican National Convention Hall. Plan.

96. Republican National Convention Hall, St. Louis. Original design.

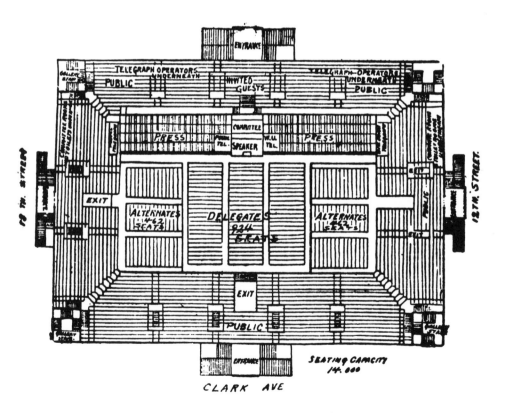

97. Republican National Convention Hall. Plan.

98. Isaiah Temple, Chicago.

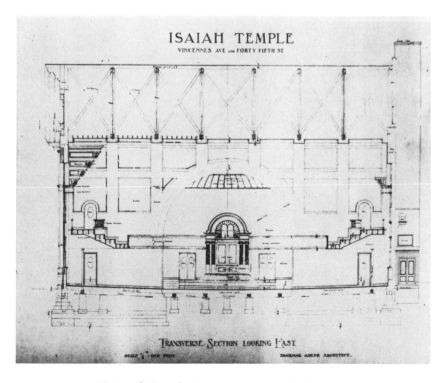

99. Isaiah Temple. Transverse section looking east.

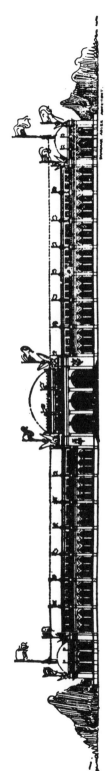

100. Exposition Building, Chicago, Elevation.

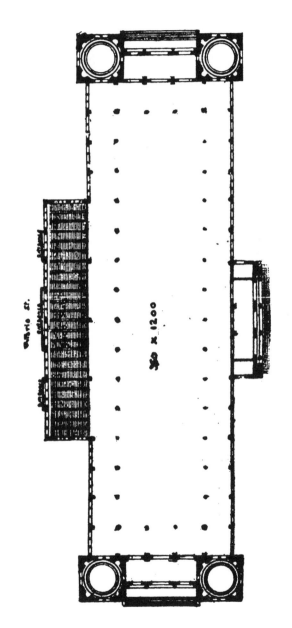

101. Exposition Building. Plan.

APPENDIX

THE CHICAGO AUDITORIUM by Dankmar Adler

Note: This paper was originally published in the Architectural Record, *vol. 1, no. 4, April–June 1892, pp. 415–434.*

The Auditorium Building illustrates how the versatile Western American can combine sentiment with thrift, and demonstrates how he can endeavor to cultivate the service of Mammon simultaneously with an effort to attain his higher artistic ideals. The wish of Chicago to possess an Opera House larger and finer than the Metropolitan, a hall for great choral and orchestral concerts, a mammoth ball-room, a convention hall, an auditorium for mass meetings, etc., etc., all under the same roof and within the same walls, gave birth to the auditorium proper. The desire that the Auditorium be made self-sustaining, and not like the Metropolitan Opera House, a perpetual financial burden to its owners, rendered necessary the external subordination of the Auditorium itself to the business building and hotel, which, together with it, form the Auditorium Building.

When the design of the Auditorium Building was first intrusted to its architects only two-thirds of the ground and less than one-half of the money finally absorbed by the work, were placed at their disposal. But, little by little, the enthusiasm of Mr. Ferd. W. Peck, the chief promoter of the enterprise, met with such response from the businessmen of Chicago as to warrant the acquisition of greater area for the building site and expansions of scope and scale far beyond the limits contemplated in the conception and development of the original design.

The form in which we find this building is, therefore, the resultant of many conflicting causes and influences. At first glance it may seem a most delightful state of things for the architects of a great building to be compelled by force of circumstances to erect a larger and more costly structure than that called for by the first instructions of their client. But the situation appears far from delightful when viewed more subjectively. After months of arduous toil the many conflicting conditions of the various problems have been harmonized and adjusted to each other, and the many thoughts brought forth by their study have been crystallized into a complete and well-rounded design and expressed in nearly two hundred plans and diagrams. Presto! The conditions change!! All that has been so laboriously thought out and so carefully adjusted must be retraversed and readjusted; not once, but a score of times; in fact, for each successive widening of the financial horizon of the enterprise. While there is an obvious gratification and pleasure in the consciousness of the widening of one's opportunities, yet this pleasure may be bought at too high a price. Such was the case with some of the developments in the growth of the design of the Auditorium, particularly after building operations had been fairly inaugurated and many conditions had thereby become fixed and inflexible.

But we are dealing with the Auditorium as it is; not with the Auditorium as it might have been had the original project been carried out, nor as it would have been had the final intentions and resources of its owners been known to its architects at the outset.

Considering first the exterior of the building; it is found dignified, impressive, simple and straightforward. Every square foot of street exposure serves commercial purposes, and serves them well. Utilitarian interests have nowhere been sacrificed, not even in the great tower, which, primarily conceived, without thought of its commercial utilization, as a means of indicating the main entrance of the Auditorium and giving it accent and emphasis in an expanse of utilitarian frontage, is now filled from cellar to roof with hotel rooms, and with offices which extend even into the machicolated cornice. Still one sees that the auditorium is not an ordinary business building, but that its exterior is the embodiment of something nobler and higher than the desire to erect an inclosure for a rent-trap.

As the Auditorium, as such, nowhere penetrates to the street fronts, but is surrounded and surmounted by office building, hotel, etc., the wants and peculiarities of these became dominant in determining the fenestration, and with it the general expression of the exterior. It is to be regretted that the severe simplicity of treatment rendered necessary by the financial policy of the earlier days of the enterprise, the deep impression made by Richardson's "Marshall Field Building" upon the Directory of the Auditorium Association and a reaction from a course of indulgence in the creation of highly decorative effects on the part of its architects should have happened to coincide as to time and object, and thereby deprived the exterior of the building of those graces of plastic surfaces decoration which are so characteristic of its internal treatment.

In taking up the consideration of the interior, the office building presents no features worthy of especial remark, except perhaps regret that it should have been pressed to completion so long in advance of other parts of the structure as to deny it a share of the richer material of finish and the more elaborate detail accorded to the hotel and auditorium.

The hotel is in one sense a marvel of planning. It is only a fringe, showing a street frontage of 587 feet with an average depth of but 45 feet skirting two sides of the auditorium, the predominant claims of which for space absorb the area usually devoted to the "working department" of hotels. The difficulties arising therefrom appear to have been overcome, for space has been found for kitchen, laundry, bakery, store-rooms and the other adjuncts of the hotel. All appear to be conveniently located and to communication with each other and with the parts of the hotel which they are intended to serve. Despite the limitation of space incident to the peculiar formation of the site, the hotel contains a number of public rooms of decided architectural pretensions and character. The main dining room in the tenth story is architecturally noteworthy.

Its ceiling is a barrel vault, divided into panels by the arched top chords of the supporting roof trusses, in which are set incandescent electric lights as an important part of the decoration. The vault is intersected in each panel by two lunettes which, however, are rather bald in treatment. They should have had sculptured or painted decorations in keeping with the mural paintings in the large segmental tympani at the ends of the barrel vault.

The banquet hall is an unusually interesting room, not only because of its construction and location, which is over the auditorium, between trusses of 118 feet span, but also because of its peculiar artistic conception and treatment, at once aggressively unconventional and original and still extremely delicate and refined. In fact, the banquet hall is the culmination of the boldness, originality and refinement which are characteristic of the decoration of this building.

The hotel office, the restaurant, the cafe and the main parlor are all rooms worthy of notice and study. The latter, 45 × 95 feet in size, is remarkable because of its connection with a loggia extending along its entire frontage, giving a most interesting outlook upon Michigan Avenue, the lake front and over Lake Michigan.

In its construction the hotel presents many interesting features. As a multiplicity of pillars would have been objectionable in the public rooms which occupy the first story of the Congress street front, and which were intended in the original design to take up all of the second floor of the same, the floors from the first story upward are carried on 140 riveted girders 2 feet high and of 36 feet clear span each. The front on which these girders occur is 360 feet long and being but 40 feet deep, is given lateral stiffness by four heavy brick walls extending from bottom to top of building. The absence of the interior columns resulting from the use of the girder construction permitted a degree of freedom in the handling of partitions and the division into rooms that was found quite useful.

The most daring and conspicuously successful structural features of the hotel are the truss constructions of 118 feet span carrying the banquet hall, weighing 660 tons, over the auditorium, and those carrying the stage, with a span of 110 feet, a load of 2,500 tons composed of stage machinery, rigging-loft, fly-galleries and four stories of hotel rooms and working departments, all of fire-proof construction. None of these were contemplated in the original plans of the building or prepared for in its foundations. The modest eight-story European hotel first contemplated would have been amply served by the present restaurant and by auxiliary eating halls intended to have been located above the same in the second story. With the increase in area and height of the building came the necessity for a large table d'hote dining-room and for the banquet hall, as well as for the enlarged kitchen, storeroom, servants' quarters, etc., etc. The dining-room itself was placed in the tenth story, with a frontage of 187 feet toward Lake Michigan, while the space required for all of the others could only be secured over the ceilings of the auditorium and stage. An effort was made, by the introduction of long beams and rails in the walls, to distribute this unexpected additional load, as far as possible, over walls and foundations. Eleven auxiliary trusses of from 75 to 118 feet span were constructed, and connected with the original roof trusses with the utmost care as regards general design and detail, and then protected against injury from fire by incombustible non-conducting inclosures of porous terra cotta and plastering upon wire cloth.

Another remarkable piece of construction is a trussed girder of 40 feet span carrying a centre load of 230 tons in the second story over the main staircase of the hotel. This, however, seems to have been uncalled for. Equally good results as to plan and artistic design could have been attained without the structural complications resulting from the omission of the pillars whose work this girder is intended to do.

The Auditorium proper, with its accessories, occupies an area of 35,800 square feet, out of a total area of 63,500 feet for the site of the building. Its cubic contents are 2,800,000 cubic feet out of a total of 8,300,000 feet for the entire building. Its general dimensions are 118 by 246 feet. To this must be added the spaces occupied for entrances and exits, for parlors and smoking-room, organ chamber and stage dressing-rooms, which encroach upon and penetrate the surrounding business and hotel buildings, some in one story only, others through from two to six stories. Again stair and elevator shafts of the business buildings and hotel make encroachments upon the auditorium. These overlappings and interpenetrations form a Chinese puzzle which cannot be understood unless illustrated by a complete set of plans and sections. On the main floor the stage occupies a depth of 70 feet, the orchestra 12 feet, the parquette 104 feet and the main foyer 60 feet. The main floor contains about 1,400 seats, arranged in generous sweeping curves and stepped up upon the lines of Scott Russell's isacoustic curve, with a total rise of 17 feet. Advantage is taken of this rise to obtain under the higher parts of the parquette an entrance foyer 80 × 118 feet, and a series of wardrobe and cloak rooms of quite generous capacity. These are at the end of the auditorium, partly under the parquette, opening from the entrance foyer and extending along both sides of the parquette. On the outside of the same are corridors 14 feet wide.

This unusually great rise of the main floor has also made practicable the arrangement of six entrances, similar to the "vomitoria" of the Roman amphitheatre, by which the lower half of the parquette seats are reached without rendering it necessary to climb to the upper level of the main floor. Excessive crowding upon the main stairs is also avoided. The boxes, forty in number, are arranged in two tiers upon each side of the parquette. The lower tier forms an arcade of semi-circular arches with rather light treatment and but little effect of enclosure, while the upper boxes are entirely open. In fact, there is nothing at all of the boxlike and stuffy effect produced by the conventional treatment of the open box. When these boxes are filled with richly dressed women, the mass effect of the rich colors and stuffs is exceedingly fine and blends quite harmoniously with the forms of the architectural detail and the colors of the decorations.

The main balcony, elliptical in plan, is 80 feet deep at the end, but quite narrow at the sides. It covers the main foyer and overhangs the parquette 20 feet at the end, but is not wide enough at the sides to completely cover the boxes. The seats are also arranged on the lines of the Scott Russell isacoustic curve, which here develops into a rise of about 40 feet from the lowest to the highest seat. Advantage has been taken of this to form two foyers, of which the lower one is 40 and the upper one 20 feet wide. Both have ample retiring and cloak rooms for the exclusive use of the occupants of the balcony. This balcony contains about 1,600 seats, the lower two-thirds of which are reached through twelve "vomitoria" opening out of the balcony foyers. The upper part of the balcony has no foyer, but free communication is established by a broad cross aisle.

Above the balcony are two galleries, each with about 500 seats. The second gallery is not over but in front of the first gallery, advantage having been taken of the favorable sight lines, due to the great depth of the house, to interpose the second gallery between the first gallery and the stage. Approach to the second gallery is had by way of horizontal bridges from the first gallery.

It will be seen from the foregoing that the Auditorium contains (including the boxes) 4,200 seats. Among the various uses to which the house is applied are many which do not require so great a seating capacity. Arrangements for reducing the size of the house have therefore been made by providing over each of the two galleries a section of movable ceiling, hung on hinges at one side and on chains passing over winches at the other. When the entire house is open, these sections of the gallery ceilings are turned upward on their hinges until raised so as to fold into panels provided for the purpose in the ceiling decoration. When it is desired to shut out either gallery from the house, these sections of their respective ceilings are lowered and turned downward on their hinges until the lower edges come down to the gallery railings, which are especially prepared for their reception. The lowered portions of the ceiling then form part of the general ceiling treatment of the hall, and the galleries are entirely shut off without impairment of the general architecture or decorative effect. If still further reduction of seating capacity is required, it is effected by a system of vertical curtains between the pillars on the line of the middle of the main balcony, by which means a further reduction in seating capacity of about 700 seats can be effected, so that when reduced to its smallest dimensions the house will contain but 2,500 seats. On the other hand, increased seating capacity for conventions, etc., is obtained by continuing the stepping of the parquette seats into the main foyer, by forming two floors of seating upon the stage, by reseating the boxes and the box corridors, etc., until a total capacity of 7,000 seats is reached. Throughout this article capacity refers to numbered seats, and is independent of standing room, etc.

The dimensions of the stage are 70 × 110 feet. The height from the floor to the rigging loft is 95 feet. The stage floor is divided into sections, all of which are separately or jointly movable in the vertical plane. This movement is effected by twenty hydraulic jacks, the plungers of which range from 6 to 24 inches in diameter and which are operated under a pressure of 100 pounds per square inch. The valves controlling these jacks are concentrated in such a manner that the person operating them is always in communication with and under the control of the stage manager. The possible downward movement from the stage floor varies for different parts of the stage from 8 feet 6 inches to 18 feet 6 inches, and the range of movement above stage level is for parts of the stage as much as 18 feet. It is possible with this apparatus to create variations and graduations of level of stage floor almost instantaneously in any direction, up or down or oblique, for any part of the stage floor. Simulations of steps, terraces, rocks, hills, caves, pits, can be produced by the mere movement of a few levers. So also can wavelike or rocking motions of greater or smaller portions of the stage floor be effected in open scene. This hydraulic apparatus is modeled upon that patented by the "Asphalia," of Vienna, and applied by it in the opera houses of Buda-Pesth, Prague and Halle. The ingenuity of American builders of hydraulic elevators and the special conditions prevailing in this building have, however, caused the introduction of many improvements and modifications of the European apparatus.

It has been stated that parts of the stage have a downward movement of 18 feet 6 inches. This brings the floor of the cellar under the stage to a general depth of 6 feet below high water of Lake Michigan, or to 4 feet below the average level of the surface of the lake. Four pits, of an area of about 150 square feet each, extend still 30 inches deeper for the purpose of receiving the framework of the lowered platforms. As the stage is only about one thousand feet distant from Lake Michigan and the intervening soil is a mixture of clay, sand and water, the influx of this water had to be guarded against. This was accomplished by excavating under the entire area of the stage to a depth averaging 3 feet below that of the finished floor. A sump had first been dug to a somewhat greater depth and the excavation kept free from water by the action of a steam pump. A thin bed of concrete was first spread over the entire surface. This was covered with a layer of Trinidad asphalt one inch thick. Over this were laid four sheets of heavy felt paper, each well saturated with asphaltum. These were again covered with an inch of asphalt. At all the edges abutting against the inclosing walls the asphalt and the felt are carried up to the high water level. To resist the upward pressure due to a possible head of over 8 feet of water the asphalt was covered with Portland cement concrete and steel rails of aggregate weight somewhat in excess of that represented by the aggregate water pressure over the entire area of the excavated space and of sufficient transverse strength to take care of the irregularities of strain caused by the varying depths of the different parts of the cellar. Where the asphalt and felt are turned up at the enclosing walls they are held in place by special retaining walls calculated with reference to the hydraulic head to be resisted. The area so treated is nearly 8,000 square feet. The treatment has been entirely successful. There have been two leaks, one caused by the breakage of a pipe, brought about by the settlement of a wall, the other caused by the melting of asphalt next to an enclosing wall, due to the proximity of the furnace of one of the steam boilers. Both leaks were stopped without difficulty and before any damage had been done by the inflowing water.

The hydraulic jacks which furnish the motive power for the movements of the stage floor extend from 12 to 24 feet below the cellar floor, and from 7 to 19 feet below the foundations of the surrounding walls. The shafts containing these hydraulic jacks were cut through a soft and treacherous soil, some almost adjacent to foundations loaded full up to the extreme bearing capacity of the soil. The shafts were polygonal in plan, lined with 8 × 8 inch timbers cut to fit accurately at the angles and inserted from below, around the excavation as rapidly as the same progressed, and carefully wedged in, layer after layer. Whenever necessary a steam pump was used to free them from water. After the shafts were completed the foot of each was filled with concrete, the cast-iron cylinders were set, and after being fixed in proper position in both the vertical and horizontal planes, the spaces between the cylinders and the shaft walls were filled with sand. With the exception of a movement sympathetic with that of the foundations of adjacent walls, the shafts and cylinders are in the position and condition in which they were originally set. The movement due to the compression of soil under wall foundations was to a great extent anticipated, and arrangements for compensation for the same, by wedges and screws, were part of the design. Of the two floors below the stage, so much as is not required for the movable parts of the stage floor and the mechanism connected therewith, is utilized for dressing rooms, store rooms, workshops, etc., the entire construction being of incombustible material, except only the floor of the stage proper, and of the intermediate stage and traps, all of which is made of 3 inch plank. On this stage there are no "sky borders," and in fact no "borders" or "flies" of any kind. The entire stage is surrounded by the "horizon," which is a panoramic representation of the sky in every gradation from clear to extreme cloudiness. These gradations are painted on an endless canvas, so mounted and attached to a special mechanism, that changes of sky effects can be made in open scene, either gradually or quickly as the action of the play demands. All scenic effects are produced by drops extending across the entire stage, perforated where necessary, and so treated as regards perspective effect as to produce all the illusions of closed stage setting.

All of these drops as well as the border lights are counterbalanced so that they can be raised or lowered from the stage floor, and not from the fly galleries. The fly galleries are utilized as stations for light effects and for storage of scenery. Fly galleries, as well as rigging loft, are built entirely of iron, the floors being made of iron strips $3/16 \times 2$ inches, placed one inch apart and riveted to the floor beams. All suspension ropes for drops, etc., are of steel, and all sheaves are of cast iron. Even the battens to which the drops are fastened are made of iron, the only combustible used in connection with stage construction and mechanism being the cables by means of which the counterweights of the drops and the drops themselves are raised and lowered.

As the curtain opening which is required for scenic presentation upon the stage is but 47 feet, while for choral concerts, conventions, balls, etc., a much greater opening is desirable, there has been provided to meet this exigency, what has been called "the reducing curtain." This is an iron framework 75 feet wide and 40 feet high, covered with plastering on wire cloth richly ornamented on the side facing the audience. Within this reducing curtain there is an opening 47 feet wide and 35 feet high. The smaller opening within the reducing curtain is closed by an iron curtain of ordinary make, and within this is the regular drop curtain of silk embroidered with gold thread. The reducing curtain weighs 10½ tons and the small iron curtain weighs 5 tons. For raising and lowering each of the three curtains there is a separate hydraulic apparatus, also for the horizon and for the paint bridge. The valves regulating all of these are on the stage within easy control of the stage manager. On both sides of the stage, to a height of four stories above and two stories below the same, are dressing rooms, and the space between the ceiling of the auditorium and its roof is utilized for the storage of scenery, properties, etc., the iron trusses being protected from fire by coverings of porous terra-cotta.

Turning now to the consideration of the artistic development of the interior of the Auditorium proper we find that the color scheme of the decoration is extremely simple. The prevailing tone is ivory—gold leaf has been liberally used in connection with the same. The plastic decoration is either shaded as old ivory or incrusted with gold.

Over the proscenium arch is a painting in the nature of a processional, the figures being life size upon a background of gold. Upon the walls enclosed by a framework of architectural forms are two large paintings. All three of these paintings are illustrations of passages in Mr. Sullivan's essay on "Inspiration," read before the Western Association of Architects some years ago. The entire color effect is at once rich, quiet and delicate. It is carried through lobbies, foyers, retiring rooms, etc., and is repeated in the Recital Hall—a small concert hall seating 500 people, placed above the auditorium.

The architectural and decorative forms found in the auditorium are unconventional in the extreme and are determined to a great extent by the acoustic effects to be attained. Hence the house is low—lowest at the stage end, thence flaring outward and upward to the extreme width and height of the room. The surfaces of the walls and ceiling are well broken. A series of concentric elliptic arches effect the lateral and vertical expansion from the proscenium opening to the body of the house. The soffits and faces of these elliptic surfaces are ornamented in relief, the incandescent electric lamps and the air inlet openings of the ventilating system forming an essential and effective part of the decoration.

The elliptic curves of the balcony are complementary to those of the ceiling. As the ceiling finally resolves itself into rectilinear forms these are taken up, and, when the galleries are shut off, continued by the fronts of the two galleries. The fronts of the galleries and balcony have a plastic treatment accentuated by groups of incandescent lamps which continue the effect of the ceiling illumination and decoration. The organ occupies on one side of the house the space ordinarily given up to proscenium boxes. The organ pipes are concealed by two grilles and a colonnade. The arrangement and treatment seem quite spontaneous and do not betray the fact that up to the time when the walls had been carried 30 feet high and the architecture and decoration of the interior drawn, it had only been intended to have a small stage organ concealed somewhere in the "flies." Still, not only has the organ been made to play an important part in the architecture of the house, but room has been found for its 7,000 pipes, and its bellows, also for its complicated electric mechanisms, for the carillons, drums, echo organ, etc., the chimes in one of the fly galleries, the echo organ between ceiling and roof at the farthest end of the house.

Much attention has been paid to the heating, cooling and ventilating apparatus. Fresh air, taken from the top of the building, is forced into the house by a fan having a wheel 10 feet in diameter and 4 feet 6 inches in face. The fresh air comes down through a shaft in which it is subjected to the action of a heavy spray. This, at all seasons of the year, washes from the air much of the dust and soot with which it is charged. In winter, warm brine is used to prevent the shower from freezing. In summer from twelve to twenty tons of ice are used for cooling the shower and with it the air. Salt is mixed with the melting ice to still further lower the temperature. For warming the air in winter it is carried through steam coils so subdivided and provided with valves that very minute gradations of temperature can be affected. A system of ducts carries the air into the different parts of the auditorium, to the stage and to the various corridors, foyers and dressing rooms. The general movement of air is from the stage outward and from the ceiling downward. The air is removed from the house by the operation of three disk fans, two of 8 feet diameter and one 6 feet in diameter. Ducts are carried to these exhaust fans from openings in the risers of all the steppings for the seats throughout the house, and from registers in every foyer, corridor, cloak room, dressing room, toilet room, etc.

Besides this main ventilating apparatus there are ten smaller fans used for the ventilation of the engine rooms, stores, kitchens, laundries, banquet hall, bath rooms, water closets, etc. Especially noteworthy is an exhaust fan, connected by means of suitable ducts with every one of the four hundred rooms containing plumbing fixtures in the hotel.

But a description of the machinery plant in ever so sketchy a manner would far exceed the possible limits of any magazine article. A mere enumeration of the parts of the same will convey an idea of the difficulties encountered by its designers. There are in use eleven boilers, capable of evaporating 54,000 pounds of water per hour, the equivalent of 1,800 horse power. There are fourteen steam engines, aggregating 1,200 horse power capacity. Of these, three serve for driving fans and laundry machinery while eleven are used for generating electric current, there being the same number of dynamos, which furnish current for over one thousand lamps and for fifteen electric motors of which eleven are used for driving fans, two for the organ, the other in connection with kitchen mechanisms. There are in the building ten passenger and four freight elevators; all hydraulic power for the same being generated by four compound duplex pumps. For pumping drinking water there are six pumps; for boiler feed and for raising water of condensation, seven pumps; and for the air washing apparatus, one pump, a total of eighteen pumps of various sizes. There are also seven hydraulic motors for driving such mechanisms as ice crushers, knife cleaners, etc. The entire apparatus is divided into two separate and distinct plants, one for the hotel only and the other for the auditorium and the business building combined. The heating apparatus of both plants is so arranged and connected that the exhaust steam is fully utilized. This is so effectively done that in cold weather steam is rarely seen escaping from the exhaust pipes, all being utilized and condensed in the heating coils and radiators. Circulation through the miles of pipes is maintained with a back pressure upon the cylinders, never yet exceeding three pounds per square inch, and in the early days of the apparatus, before the gradients of the pipes had been disturbed by settlements of the building, with a back pressure of less than one pound per square inch. An object of interest is the switch-board on the stage of the auditorium, which controls and regulates 4,000 lamps. This is set behind the reducing curtain and is hung on hinges in such manner that when the reducing curtain is down and the house is used as an opera house or theatre, the switch-board is to the right of the curtain opening, as in all theatres. When the stage is to be widened, the switch-board is turned outward 90 degrees so as to leave clear the entire opening of 75 feet, produced by raising the reducing curtain.

But there has been enough discursive statement of details of arrangement, construction and appointment, and it remains only to summarize briefly the results achieved.

Regarding business building, hotel and external treatment enough has already been said. There remain the Auditorium proper in its relations to its various purposes and the structural and the financial problems and their solutions.

Before disposing of the Auditorium proper, attention must again be called to the reducing curtain and its functions. For operatic and dramatic performances, for lectures and for concerts not involving the use of a mass chorus the reducing curtain is down and the house is simply a mammoth theatre or opera house with a proscenium or curtain opening of 47 feet. When, however, the house is used for a concert by a great chorus, for a political convention, a hall or a fair, the reducing curtain is raised and the entire stage becomes part of the auditorium. The chorus seats rise tier upon tier 75 feet wide, 70 feet deep, closed in on the sides with suitable decorations and covered with a series of sounding boards suspended from the rigging loft. If used for a ball the entire parquette, orchestra and stage are floored over and the stage enclosed by a continuous set scene in panoramic form, apparently a continuation of the arcade formed by the lower boxes, the arches filled with tropical foliage and flowers, in the centre of which is the orchestra. The arrangement for conventions has already been referred to.

The success of the room is greatest when used as a hall for mass concerts. The chorus seems thus to blend with the audience, and the house is so open that one can see at a glance almost the entire audience and the whole chorus. The sight of thousands of men and women in festive array is always pleasing, and when every one of these has ample space for sitting in comfort, has fresh air and can see and be seen and hear every modulation of sound in its full effect the result is inspiring. But little less effective and successful is the Auditorium as an opera house.

The stage settings are generally complete and sumptuous, the effect of the music as perfectly transmitted to the farthest corners of the house as the most critical can wish. It should here also be stated that the value of the stage appointments and mechanisms asserts itself at every performance. With stage hands one-third in number of those required for similar work in the Metropolitan Opera House all changes and transformations are made quickly and smoothly and there has never yet been a case when the actors have waited for the stage. On the contrary, the stage is always set before the actors or singers have made their changes of costume, etc.

All of this is, of course, also of value for dramatic performances, of which there has been a number of successful ones in the house, the two galleries being shut off. While the actors were easily heard and understood in every part of the house, objection was made by many to the fact that distance from the stage made observation of play of features too difficult for full enjoyment of the performance. As a hall for orchestral concerts or for virtuosi on individual instruments the hall has proved all that would be wished for, as also for use as a lecture hall. Its effect as a ball-room is almost that of fairy land, and as a convention hall it permits every spectator to see and hear all that is being said and done upon the platform, and would in this particular also seem to have fulfilled its purpose were it not for the demand in the case of National Nominating Conventions for a greater seating capacity.

The many peculiarities of the hall in acoustic properties, brilliancy of illumination, purity of atmosphere, conveniences of ingress and egress, comfort of seats, number, size, and elegance of foyer, promenades, etc., and the many coat-rooms, retiring and toilet-rooms, etc., distributed throughout all parts of the house, all these assert themselves in each of the many uses for which the Auditorium has been built, and leave no doubt of its unqualified success and show that it fulfills the expectations of its founders.

As to the success of the building considered as a piece of architectural engineering, the verdict while in the main favorable, must be qualified by the regret that the preparations for resisting the strains caused by the growth of the building into larger proportions and heavier weights than at first contemplated had not been confined to the superstructure, but had been begun with the foundations. But as this could not have been expected under the conditions prevailing, the visible effects of certain irregularities of settlement of foundations must be considered as the price paid for many admirable features in the completed building, which had been deemed financially unattainable when the foundations were designed and built.

The problems in steam, mechanical and hydraulic, engineering have been successfully solved. The only difficulties encountered in the practical operation of the plant were remedied without great labor or expense. It may interest many to know that the source of complaint was the noise produced by the rush of large columns of water under great head through the supply pipes of the Tower Elevator. This was remedied by substituting a compression tank for the gravity tank as a source of water supply for these elevators. Another was the difficulty of maintaining the water column in the long suction pipes of the elevator, the service of which was from the nature of the case very irregular. In the case of one set of pumps a special contrivance for "priming" was provided, in the case of the other the tank was raised above the level of the pump valves. Minor difficulties in regulating air supply from and to fans were remedied by readjustment of dampers, valves, etc.

In quite a number of instances the folly of a municipal regulation prescribing vent pipes for traps was demonstrated. Owing to the great height of the building the friction of the air in these vent pipes became so great that they failed to do their intended duty. "Sanitas" and other anti-siphoning traps were substituted for the S traps, and the inoperative trap vents were disconnected, since which there has been no further trouble.

The two electric light and power plants, each at the time of its construction the largest in the world, were really an evolution brought about by a series of experimental efforts which after many vexatious failures finally produced an efficient and easily controlled apparatus.

Whether or not the enterprise is an unqualified financial success can hardly be definitely stated. So much, however, is certain: Chicago has an Auditorium far better as an opera house or a concert hall or a ballroom than either the Metropolitan Opera House or the Music Hall of New York, and the certainty that its owners will not be assessed to assure its maintenance is already established beyond the possibility of doubt. That a dividend will be realized upon the investment is more than probable. Time is, however, required for a southward movement of the business centre of Chicago sufficient to fill all the stores and offices with tenants at rentals approximating those paid in similar premises a few blocks north of the Auditorium. Even now there is a small surplus revenue, which, however, is being applied to the payment of a floating debt incurred by reason of the failure of the management to dispose of a part of its capital stock which is still held in the treasury.

THE THEATRE by Dankmar Adler

Note:

Adler was working on this paper at the time of his death. The various notes which have survived (donated by Joan W. Saltzstein to the Newberry Library, Chicago) indicate the paper never reached the stage of a final version, but its full content had been established. Certain portions were rewritten several times. There are, therefore, several versions of these sections. In some cases the only clue as to when various manuscripts belong together is their subject matter.

In order to assist the reader in determining how this paper has been reconstructed, a note in parentheses has been placed at the end of each section to indicate from which manuscript that section was taken. The manuscripts, therefore, have been assigned a letter (based only on the order in which they appear here). When a series of notes for the same section exists and a progression of revisions was evident, the final revision is that which was used. In revising his notes, on one occasion Adler removed a statement which he apparently felt to be extraneous to his paper, but which might be of interest to the modern reader. It has been included and noted as such. No changes have been made in the paragraph construction, punctuation, grammar, or vocabulary—only spelling errors have been corrected.

A shorter and rather different version of this paper, edited by Rachel Baron, appeared in The Prairie School Review, *vol. 2, no. 2, Second Quarter, 1965, pp. 21–27. A biography of Adler in* The Reform Advocate *of May 4, 1901, page 389, indicates this paper was to have appeared in an architectural encyclopedia to be published by Macmillan and Company. This was likely the* Dictionary of Architecture and Building *by Russell Sturgis published by Macmillan in 1901. Although this work contains a reference to the isacoustic curve, the principle which Adler considered essential to the design of theatres, it does not contain any material written by him.*

The art of designing theatres, as exemplified by those built up to the beginning of the last part of the nineteenth century, has not reached the standard attained for man's other achievements in carrying out his manifest destiny; the subjugation of the materials and forces of nature to his uses.

The designers of bridges, ships, and machines must foretell with accuracy the structural and economic results expected from their works. If these works fail under stress of actual service to fulfill their predicted performances, the modern world has no use for them and no place for their authors.

Not so in the case of a theatre. Not all of those who occupy its seats may be able to see, few may be able to hear that which is presented upon the stage. Yet theatres in which these things are experienced are considered normal, and when a theatre is found in which all can see and hear, such result is received by the public contemporaneous with the publication of this work as something abnormal; as a phenomenon, the repetition of which is not to be expected by the interposition of another lucky chance.

It should not be more difficult to predict the behavior of sound waves within a theatre than it is to determine the interactions of sea waves, ship, and propelling screws, or the conduct of steam in the cylinders of an engine, or the frequency and intensity of the pulsations of electric energy as it leaves a generator or enters a motor; and when compared with the conservation of sound and its transmission to distant space through the telephone, or into time and space by means of the phonograph, how trifling are the problems of sound control and transmission within the enclosing walls of a theatre.

But theatre building is old. It has a history as well as traditions and superstitions whose baneful influence upon contemporaneous theatre design, like many an other architectural aberration, is the result of a mental attitude which sees in a brilliant and admirable achievement of the past, not a legitimate evolution from the conditions of its own environment, but a creation standing out for all ages to be blindly idolized and imitated. Were our mental vision trained to take note, not merely of the Historical in architecture, we should perceive that all structures owe their origin to evolutionary spiritual forces and processes, living for all time, changing and adapting themselves to and working with and through each successive phase of environment of the human race, and not embalmed or rigidly crystallized in the structures to which they have given being.

Therefore, strictly speaking, the true history of architecture is the history of the evolution of human civilization, and each structure which has been conceived and reared by man is but the visible manifestation of a phase of that evolution. This is the spirit in which the author of this article sees the theatre that has been, the theatre that is, and the theatre that should be.

Taking the history of the theatre in its narrower sense, and endeavoring to trace it to its beginning, we find that the span of time between the dawn of man's first efforts at histrionic presentations, and the Coliseum is but partially bridged over by records and ruins left for our examination; and that another chapter of history as interesting, and in the earlier stages as tantalizingly obscure as that of the time which antedated the Olympic Games and the Coliseum, was begun shortly after the period when this and antecedent structures of similar character had been converted into ruins by inswarming hordes of barbarians; after which the art of producing and housing histrionic presentations had again to be conceived and developed, and whence it has been carried on to our day.

Toward the foreground of both of these periods, documentary and monumental remains became more frequent, so that the Periclean period to the shattering of Roman Civilization, and from the day of the miracle play and the great Italian Renaissance to the contemporary play house, authentic illustrations of the growth and development of the theatre of each period are within our reach.

The scope of this article precludes giving an adequate statement of these histrionic developments, but reference is made to the following works, accessible to American readers:

----

[1]

In Continental Europe, up to a comparatively recent period, theatres and opera houses were built by kings and potentates as part of the glory and splendor of their courts. Their designers found it necessary to give foremost consideration to arrangements for the display of gorgeous costumes by the court nobility. Hence the practice of surrounding each auditorium by tiers upon tiers of stalls or boxes, so disposed that the magnificence of the toilets and jewels worn by their occupants were fully in evidence, as important and essential a feature of the spectacle as the play presented upon the stage. The space thus enclosed formed a deep pit, in which the commonality and those in the lower ranks of the military were crowded together, standing or at best seated on hard benches, looked down upon by the occupants of the boxes. Finally at dizzy height, amidst the heat and vapor arising from innumerable burning candles and lamps and from the audience below, one or more narrow galleries were occupied by beings of still lesser social import than those who filled the pit of the theatre.

In England, puritanic influence prevented support of players, plays and playhouses by contributions from the public purse. There were long periods when the play was not even tolerated, and it was late in the 16th century before theatres were built in London, only to be closed half a century later by order of Parliament. These first English theatres were commercial ventures of actors, playwrights and speculating carpenters, hence cheap structures of wood and plaster, modeled upon prototypes with which their builders were familiar. These prototypes were the enclosed courtyards of inns, surrounded by galleries, the stage improvised in the center or at one side, the guests of the inn and their friends looking down from the galleries, while tradespeople and servants filled the level spaces of the court itself. Thus, when Architecture and its conventions took possession of the English theatre, it found a type of construction, crude and inelegant, yet in its general lines almost identical with the plans developed on the Continent in the style of the Renaissance and of the Rococo from the classic theatre of Vitruvius.

Hence, the beginning of this century found one type of theatre design common to the civilized world. The typical characteristics of its auditorium were: 1. level, or nearly level pit; 2. high surrounding walls masked by balconies and galleries; 3. a ceiling raised high above these high walls by the in-

terposition of an entablature or cove, or of both; 4. within the
ceiling a dome raising high enough to allow the main central
chandelier to be hung above the line of vision of the greater
part of the audience; and 5. a proscenium fashioned and decorated according to the rules conventionally accepted for the
proportions of the doorway of the period of the Renaissance.

Almost the entire nineteenth century has lapsed, and theatre design is still dominated by reverence for this historically
transmitted type, whose strongest manifestation is found in
efforts to fashion with historical correctness and academic accuracy the proportions of the proscenium opening.

Neither historical nor conventionally esthetic considerations justify the use of forms and types not adapted to the ful-
fillment of actual and practical requirements, but the exis-
tence of the latter should be proved before the former are set
aside. The following summary of the essential conditions un-
derlying theatre design is therefore given as justification of
advocacy of another, not an historical basis for the theories
hereinafter stated.

Without a play to be produced upon the stage there will not
be a theatre. When there is nothing which excites a desire to
see and hear a performance, there will be no spectators and
no audience. If the actors are hampered in their work by faults
and imperfections of stage construction and equipment, they
may be unable to render the play in a manner which attracts
the public and stimulates attendance. Therefore, no theatre
design can be considered as fulfilling legitimate requirements unless there has been consideration of and provision
for everything which furthers scenic illusion, facilitates
movement upon the stage, and makes for the comfort and
convenience of actors and all others employed upon the
stage. Yet after all this has been done, if the spectators are not
so disposed that each can see every setting, if every member of
the audience is not able to hear distinctly and without effort
every word spoken upon the stage, then no matter how con-
summate the art of the performers, the structure will not have
fulfilled its purpose.

Among the circumstances and conditions which effect the
construction and equipment of *the stage,* are the following:

The stage may be used for the presentation of a play whose scene of action is in forest or prairie, in mid-ocean or on mountain-top, in palace, cathedral or cottage, in narrow street or spacious plaza. Its time of action may be night or day, summer or winter, in fair weather or in foul, under bright sunshine or lowering storm. The action upon the stage may be the delivery of a monologue or the rioting of a mob, the billing and cooing of a pair of lovers or the maneuverings of an army. Change and transformation from extreme to extreme may occur several times in a single play, or as in many of the older plays, even in the course of a single act.

The proscenium opening forms the frame through which the audience views stage setting and action, and determines the dimension of the stage picture seen by the audience.

The stage picture cannot be made larger than its frame, but it is often reduced to smaller dimensions by the use of appliances called "tormenter wings" and "valence drops", which are interposed between the proscenium proper and the stage picture. Later in this article the subject of dimensions of proscenium opening will be taken up in conjunction with the discussion of optic and acoustic requirements.

Turning now to the stage picture within the proscenium opening, we find that except in rare instances, and only upon a comparatively small scale, it is impossible to present an actual reproduction of the scenes and objects, structures and localities among and within which the scene of action of the play is laid, and that they must therefore be shown in pictorial presentment; whence the necessity that each stage must contain the component parts of many stage pictures, so contrived and so disposed that many changes of scene may be presented in rapid succession. Therefore lightness and compactness are essential qualities of the medium in which these pictures are rendered. Experience has shown that these and other necessary qualities are found in large sheets of painted canvas.

Among the most effective means of forming stage pictures is a succession of painted curtains called "drops", of which the hindmost forms a picture background which occupies the entire back of the stage. Between the back drop and the proscenium are placed other drops, the sides and top of which are painted as part of the perspective of the stage picture, the interior being cut out to allow for the movement of

197

stage action. For the presentation of small interiors, rooms actually constructed of canvas walls and ceiling upon which the perspective effects are properly painted may take the place of drops. Combination of drops and smaller pieces of scenery, moveable in a horizontal direction are also used. The smaller pieces of scenery are handled directly upon the stage by the hands of the scene shifters. The drops are suspended from above, the ropes and pulleys being placed upon a grid-iron floor called the "rigging loft", which is placed at a height sufficiently elevated above the wings to allow the lifting of the drops bodily above the proscenium opening without folding or rolling of the canvas. This height equals double the height of the "drops", plus a reasonable space for the manipulation of the mechanism employed for raising and lowering. One or more galleries, also with gridiron floors, called "fly galleries" are generally found upon the sides of the stage, and from these are handled the ropes coming down from the rigging loft. The "Gridiron" type of floor is used for fly galleries and rigging loft in order to allow the passing of ropes through the openings between the floor slats. Formerly these slats were made of wood. Now many are made of heavy hoop iron, and some of combinations of metal and concrete. Here and there theatres are found in which the drops are counter balanced and here the ropes which control the movements of the counter weights are handled directly from the sides of the stage. Efforts have also been made to utilize hydraulic pressure, steam, and the electric current for effecting the movements of stage scenery.

The stage floor is now generally made level, although in older theatres there are many instances of inclined stage floors. The latter formed a partial corrective to bad sight lines, they assisted the scene painter in the working out of perspective effects, and gave a certain spring and elan to the forward movement of the ballet. With the necessity for the adaptation of the stage to the scenic requirements of many plays produced in quick succession upon its boards, and for the interchangeability of scenery and properties of different theatres, has come the general use of the level stage floor.

The exigencies of many plays require that preparation be made for effecting the appearance and disappearance through the stage floor of participants in the stage action, sometimes singly,—sometimes in groups. Hence the introduction of moveable traps and of bridges in the stage floor, the movement of which, in most stages, is effected and controlled by means of windlasses and counter-weights, and in some by means of hydraulic apparatus, and in a few by electric apparatus. Where either electric or hydraulic apparatus is used it is customary to divide the entire stage floor into sections of convenient dimensions, each made to move independently of the other, and to dispense with the building up upon the stage of platforms for the presentation of balconies, terraces, bridges, hillsides or rocks, but to effect this entirely by means of the movements of the stage floor itself into the positions required.

Light effects form a most important accessory to the successful working of the stage. It is impracticable to use sunlight. Its illuminating powers are limited by the position of the sun at the varying times of day, and by clouds, and greatly interfered with also by the artificial scenery and the structure and mechanism of the stage. What is wanted in a theatre is a means of illumination entirely within control as to intensity, color and area of effectiveness, in order that it can be used and manipulated as an adjunct to the many and varying requirements of scenic development. The illumination of the scenery must be at all times such as to produce the varying conditions of light and shade phenomenon, as observed in forest, field or mountain, and about and within the structures reared by man. And withal the illumination must be so diffused and directed as to prevent the casting of black shadows of eyebrow, nose, lips, etc., upon the faces of the participants in stage action. The stage is therefore surrounded by lamps provided with reflectors placed and set in such manner as to conceal the lamps themselves from the audience and to throw their light upon scenery and actors. When electricity is used, each set of lights is generally in triplicate, one set of bulbs white, one red, and one green. The lamps are so switched that at the pleasure of the stage manager the current can be sent through any or all of them at any time. The foot-lights are necessarily stationary. The lights at the top and sides are moveable and they are arranged in sets corresponding in number and position with the successive range of drops and borders. They are frequently hung with counter-weights so that they can be raised or lowered with the drops and borders.

In determining the dimensions of the stage, it appears that no matter how large the stage, that portion of it which is exposed to the audience can by the interposition of proper enclosing scenery be so reduced as to encompass a small space representing a small theatre of action. But no matter how clever the perspective of the scene painter, how great the ingenuity of the stage carpenter and machinist, space is required to provide the foreground necessary for the successful rendering of the perspective of the interior of a temple or cathedral, or of a great plaza, or for any of the grander phases of natural scenery. And still more difficult is it to effect in small space an illusion of the maneuverings of large bodies of men and women engaged in the action of a play. Therefore it is difficult to make a stage too large, it may easily be made too small.

In European theatres the value of space as an adjunct to successful stage presentation is fully recognized, and in the great opera houses, such as that at Paris, or Vienna, or Milan, the stage occupies an area several times greater than that of the Auditorium. Still, it must be said that for ordinary presentations but a small portion of these monster stages is used and very effective stage settings for either outdoor or interior effects have been made on the comparatively small stage characteristic of the American theatre.[2]

The auditorium of a theatre, as its name implies, is a place whose occupants have come for the purpose of hearing. Therefore, the circumstances and conditions which affect the conservation and transmission of sound as well as the peculiarities and limitations of the human ear must be dominant elements in the design of any auditorium.

When atmospheric air is made to assume a wave movement having a frequency of between _____ and _____[3] waves per second and a velocity of about 1100 feet per second, the sensation transmitted to the brain by an interposed ear is called sound, and the waves producing this phenomenon are called sound waves.

There are no recorded observations which give air an exceptional status among the substances which compose the universe. Hence in common with other substances air must be considered subject to the laws of gravitation and of the conservation of energy, and as possessing inertia; it must be assumed that its movements are accompanied and impeded by friction, that when in unobstructed motion, air waves follow the line of original impulse, that when reflected the angles of incidence and reflection of their movement are equal and that a line of least resistance is sought and followed by any air movement which meets with obstacles to its progress through space.

As we see on the surface of a pool into which a pebble has been thrown a series of concentric waves whose motion grows feebler and feebler as distance from the point of impact increases, so is the impact of a sound impulse thrust into the air followed by a series of concentric air waves encircling the line of direction of sound impulse, their progress in every direction cumulatively impeded by inertia and friction until the initial energy of the impulse has been exhausted. If a sound wave in its progress through space encounters an interposed object, changes of condition of interposed object and of original sound wave will ensue in conformity with general physical laws. Whatever these changes may be, the sum total of effect will not exceed the residuum of energy which efforts to overcome inertia and friction have left to the intercepted sound wave at the moment of contact. Therefore, the manifestations consequent upon such contact will be strongest if the interposing object is placed near the origin of sound impulse, and feeblest if it be placed at a distance from this point, the ratio of difference, by reason of cumulative effect of opposing inertia and friction, being as the squares of their respective distances.

Certain physical limitations of the auditory nerves of the average human being are important factors in the science of acoustics. Among these is the inability of the ordinary human ear to become sensitive to wave movements whose velocities differ much from 1100 feet per second and whose pulsations have a frequency less than _____ per second, or more than _____[4] per second.

If therefore, an original sound wave proceeding from any

given sound impulse strikes the ear, and reflections of other waves emanating from the same impulse strike the same ear within a period of less than one-tenth of a second, their combined effect upon the auditory nerve will be as that of one sound. Although unable under this condition to separate these individual sound manifestations, the ear cannot ignore their cumulative impact: the sensation will be stronger and louder in direct proportion to the number of sound wave impacts crowded into the period of one-tenth of a second. If, on the other hand, the time interval between impact upon the ear of original wave and of reflected waves exceeds one-tenth of a second, the sensation sent by the auditory nerve to the brain will be that of two or more sounds, neither having the cumulative strength of united effect but each strong enough to induce confusion and indistinctness. Again, if within the period of one-tenth of a second, the ear is assailed by original and reflected sound wave movements which owe their origin to two or more sound impulses then, owing to its inability to distinguish and classify wave rhythms coming so closely upon each other, the effect will be more or less approximate to unintelligibility, depending upon the number of individual sound wave movements thrust into such periods of less than one-tenth of a second. Therefore, there are two reasons for placing the sound reflecting surfaces as near the point of sound production as practicable. First, so that the waves to be reflected may retain enough of the strength of their original impulse still to be within the ear's range of perceptiveness, second, that the difference in time required by original weakly reflected sound waves to traverse these respective distances to the ear of the auditor shall be less than one-tenth of a second.

If in its progress through the air a sound wave impinges upon a substance harder than air, it will take on a sympathetic wave movement, the extent of which is proportional to the elasticity and to the density of the interposed substance. (*End of Manuscript "A"*)

When on a pool table the cue ball strikes a group of object balls, the motion imparted to all of the object balls, plus that remaining in the cue ball, represent a sum total which, less the energy expended in friction, is equal to the original energy which has set the cue ball in motion.

If one of the object balls in its motion encounters the cue ball it will accelerate the movement of the cue ball, while its own space will be correspondingly diminished.

If sound waves in their progress encounter interposed objects, such as walls, floors or ceilings, a new series of wave movements will be set up within the substances which form these surfaces, but these new wave movements will be modified in rhythm and intensity by the characteristics of structures of the materials so encountered. While traveling in these substances these wave movements will in their turn effect a movement in the surrounding air which upon reaching an ear interposed within the range of its movement will cause the sensation of sound. The new sound wave so formed will take on a quality which may differ considerably from that of the original sound wave by reason of the structural qualities and peculiarities of the solid material which has been interposed in the path of the original wave. (*From Manuscript "B"*)

If soft fluffy materials are used as intercepting media, the energy of the sound producing impulse will, to a great extent be absorbed. If the intercepting medium is very hard like stone and the surface very smooth the sound wave will be reflected in almost its full original energy. If the intercepting medium is somewhat less hard and firm in texture and at the same time elastic, like wood, part of the energy of the sound wave will expend itself in producing a sympathetic wave movement in the interposed medium, while the wave, diminished in energy by whatever of its movement has been taken up by the intercepting medium, will be reflected into space. (*From Manuscript "C"*)

Besides this difference in quality of wave movement, there is also a difference in the velocity of same as between the solid substance and the air. The effect, therefore which is produced by the impinging of a series of sound waves upon wall and ceiling of an auditorium is fully as manifold as that produced by the striking of the cue ball on a pool table against a group of object balls.

Generally speaking it may be said that the sound wave is reflected from the interposed surface back into the room but not all its energy is so reflected. Part of its force expends itself in setting up a wave movement within the substance which forms the interposed wall or ceiling. The reflected original sound wave may pass directly to the ear of one of the audience, or it may encounter another surface or object, and be again reflected.

The wave movement which is set up in the substance of the wall or ceiling will take on quality and velocity differing from those of the original sound wave and characteristic of the material of which walls and ceiling may be composed.

In the case of many substances this wave movement is strong enough to again produce sound wave movements in the adjacent ear. If the wall and ceiling surfaces are large the areas exposed to the wave making impulses of the contained air will be great, and the number of successive wave impulses given by the successive contacts of the same wave will be great and cumulative within the substance of the walls or ceiling, and again cumulative in their effect upon the surrounding air.

If these surfaces are large and the distances traversed great, the difference in rate of progress of corresponding sound waves in air and in solid will eventually become great enough to exceed one-sixth of a second, and will hence become perceptible to the ear of an auditor within the room in which this has taken place, the result being a reverberatory effect which makes for unintelligibility and confusion of sound.

This is something entirely different from the phenomenon of the echo which is found when a sound wave encounters a surface so situated that it reflects a sound directly back to the point of origin in a period of time exceeding one-sixth of a second from the time when the original sound has become sensible to the auditor.

On smoother surfaces this difference in progress of sound wave movement and action and reaction of air and enclosing surfaces invariably produces confusion of sound. If, however, the enclosing surfaces are well broken up, the floors by steps, seats, audience, etc., the walls by projects, pilasters, pillars and by galleries, and ceiling by heavy beams, arches or deep coffers, the effects of the reaction upon the air of the induced wave movement of the solid substance is broken up and cannot be sufficiently cumulative to impinge upon the ear within periods greater than one-sixth of a second apart. (*From Manuscript "B"*) *The floors, walls, and ceiling of a theatre, should, therefore*,[5] be so disposed as to prevent, as far as possible, either dissipation or premature absorption of sound wave energy, and with a view to carrying the sound waves as nearly as possible in full volume and purity, and with unimpaired distinctness to the ears of the audience.

The sounds which the audience has come to hear are produced upon the stage, but when it is attempted to provide within the limits of the stage fixed surfaces for preventing dissipation of sound waves and for reflecting them outward into the auditorium, the exigencies of stage setting are such as to leave vast open spaces but no reflecting surfaces behind, above, to right, or left of actors and singers; and even when the scene of stage action is small, the enclosing surfaces are formed of canvas from which active sound reflection cannot be expected. Therefore, the sound waves of whose movements trend toward the interior of the stage, are, to a great extent, unavailable for transmission into the auditorium, and whatever is done toward conserving and controlling the energy of the sound waves in general, will from the nature of the case, be almost wholly confined to the auditorium, and must be done with all the more care and judgment because of the unavoidable dispersion which cannot be prevented on the stage.

There will be no sound dispersion downward either on stage or in auditorium for the floor of both is so near the mouths of the speakers, singers, and musical instruments that it intercepts and reflects the sound waves long before the vigor of their original formative impulse has expended itself.

Assuming the axial line of the wave movement produced by speaker, singer, or instrument, to be drawn outward into the auditorium, one-half of the sound wave energy will be directed downward from this axial line, and the other half upward. The downward moving impulses soon strike the floor, are reflected, and join in their ceilingward movement the original half of upward tending sound waves. But the tympani of the ears which are to vibrate in harmony with the sound waves are near the floor, not at the ceiling, and those wave movements which expend their energy in efforts to reach the ceiling are lost to the audience. But if the distance to the ceiling is made small enough these upward tending sound wave movements will be arrested and reflected back toward the audience before their energy is expended in the effort to propel themselves through the air. Therefore, if sound conservation and its propulsion to where it will do most good were all that is to be attained in the design of a theatre, ceiling lines would be established at levels but little above the heads of the actors. But there are other considerations. A ceiling line so drawn would produce a sense of discomfort and oppressiveness in the minds of the audience. Again, there must be room for the formation of a stage picture. As essential portions of this may be upon the back drop, and that may be next to the back wall of the stage, no part of the ceiling which may be considered as beginning with the proscenium arch should extend below a line drawn from the eye of the highest spectator in the auditorium to the upper line of the more essential parts of the stage picture. Thus the upper line of the proscenium opening will be coincident with the lower line of the valance, which is a so well known feature in the treatment of the typical conventional theatre.

If the proscenium opening, and with, or without it, the ceiling be raised above these lines, there will be a corresponding and unnecessary dissipation of sound, and consequent impairment of acoustic qualities of the theatre.

There may be reluctance to accept as final and decisive a dictum so antagonistic to time hallowed practice. But upon reflection this reluctance cannot but disappear. The acoustically improper proportions of proscenium opening and consequent excessive ceiling height which have become characteristic of theatre design owe their origin to the fact that Vitruvius, Palladio, Vignola and other authorities knew of no wall opening except the door or window, that as the architecture of whose canons they were the expounders had established certain proportions of height to width of doors and windows, the proscenium opening must follow these proportions. Again, an opening of so great size must have the most dignified and grandiose treatment known to the style, and that implied the use of pilasters or pillars surmounted by an entablature and this again by a cove forming a background for emblematic sculpture or a field for a great decorative fresco.

When the splendors of toilets of the more important part of

the audience was displayed in many tiers of galleries, the structure as well as the decorations of these were made to blend quite naturally with the treatment of the high proscenium which in fact formed from the standpoint of decorative art, a logical and appropriate feature at once terminating the lines of the galleries and dominating the entire design. Then coming nearer home in time and place, the abhorrence of "squattiness" which forms one of the most marked traits of the attitude toward architecture of the average American, have maintained the proscenium of classical proportions curtailed from theoretical to practical limitations of height by a painted rag called a "valance".

However, as the tendency of artistic thought and development tends toward recognition of the requirements of use and service and toward willingness to accent the forms developed by practical considerations, as the basis of artistic design and decorative treatment, it is probably that the few tentative efforts which have recently been made toward adoption to acoustic requirements of proscenium opening and ceiling height of theatres will bear fruit and in after years that when future editions of this work are published the reader of this paper will deem it strange that anyone should have deemed it necessary to attack what will then have become an obsolete or at least an obsolescent practice.

While the low proscenium and ceiling contribute more than any other feature to the acoustic success of a theatre, there are many others which must not be neglected. Where walls and ceilings are smooth and unbroken, many sound waves by impact with other sound waves are thrown into lines parallel with walls and ceilings and creep along at modified speed, gathering volume by the addition of others of like character and also influenced by the vibrations of walls and ceilings they finally assume a rhythm varying from that of the waves moving freely in air, and thus blur the sensation to the auditory nerves. Therefore, it is advisable always to break up ceiling surfaces, and also the wall surfaces, unless this is already accomplished by galleries.

But little of stage setting or action can be seen by those who occupy the front side seats of a theatre. If these are cut off by walls extending from floor to ceiling and the plan of the room thus made fan shaped, its acoustic efficiency will be enhanced by reason of interception and reflection into the auditorium of sound waves which would otherwise be wasted.

The materials of which the floors, walls and ceilings of a theatre are formed are an important factor in the determination of its acoustic qualities. Large areas of very hard surfaces are formed by materials such as marble, brick, or plastering applied directly to brick, or metal, or tiles, will impart hardness and harshness of tones and are apt to engender rattling vibrations. On the other hand, drapings of woolen cloth, velvet or plush or upholstered surfaces absorb sound and fail to reflect it and thus tend to greatly diminish its volume, thereby rendering hearing difficult.

The use of resonant materials such as wood or rough plaster on metallic laths is advisable, particularly when used as wall coving if separated by an air space from the walls themselves. The value of resonance of the materials composing walls and ceiling facings seems to be due to sympathetic synchronous vibrations which are set up by impinging sound waves.

There is a configuration of the floor, which if constructed upon the lines of Scott Russell's well known "isacoustic" curve will also give "isaoptic" lines, which are of no mean importance for many people hear partly with their eyes, by watching play of features, and then of course people want to see all that is enacted upon the stage.

The isacoustic sloping of the floors is of further importance in this, that it not only removes obstacles to direct progress of sound waves to ears, but also interposes sound reflecting surfaces sooner and more effectively than would be the case were the floor either level or were it uniformly sloped.

Assuming now that every member of an audience is seated in position to hear and see with ease, that the seats and aisles are so disposed as to furnish abundant and convenient means of ingress and egress, assume that the galleries are high enough not to give a sense of confinement and oppression to those who sit below them, not yet so high as to place their occupants at too high a level above the stage, assume that the galleries come forward so as to give their occupants a sense of nearness to the stage and that the gallery projection is not so great as to block the range of vision of those who sit under the rear of it and that the illumination is at once uniform, soft and brilliant and that the lights are so disposed as not to shine into the eyes of the audience, and yet absence of suitable ventilating apparatus may prevent enjoyment of even the best of stage presentations.

An efficient system of ventilation will introduce fresh air of uniformly mild temperature and will remove foul air. Openings for admission and removal of air will be so large and so widely used, so uniformly distributed that the air movement will be constant, uniform and at moderate, scarce perceptible velocity. To promote more efficient sound transmission, the general trend of air currents will be outward and forward from the stage, particularly under all galleries. (*End of Manuscript "D"*)

1. Adler left the blanks, apparently planning to fill in the references at a later time. He never finished the task. There is no indication in his notes to which works he was referring.
2. This paragraph occurs only in an early version.
3. Adler left the blanks, apparently planning to look up the figures at a later time. He never finished the task. The correct numbers are: approximately 16 cycles and 20,000 cycles per second.
4. See note #3 above.
5. The beginning of the sentence has been reconstructed.

Index

A NOTE ABOUT THE AUTHORS

Charles E. Gregersen is the architect of a number of significant historic preservation and design projects in the greater Chicago area. He has written and lectured on various aspects of architectural history and has been actively involved in the preservation of the Pullman landmark district where he resides. The late Joan W. Salzstein was Dankmar Adler's granddaughter. She was involved in the field of architectural history as a writer, lecturer, and preservation activist.